YUDIT KISS was born in Budapest in 1956. After having worked in Hungary, Mexico and the UK, she moved to Switzerland in the early 1990s, where she currently lives. A specialist in economic development, she is the author of numerous books, research papers and academic works. *The Summer My Father Died* is her first literary work.

GEORGE SZIRTES is a celebrated poet and translator. His books include *Reel*, which won the T. S. Eliot Prize in 2004. He is also a Fellow of the Royal Society of Literature. His translations include *Metropole* by Ferenc Karinthy (Telegram, 2008).

YUDIT KISS

The Summer My Father Died

Translated from Hungarian by
George Szirtes

TELEGRAM

First published in Hungarian in 2006 as *Apám halálának nyara*
by Noran-Könyvek Kft., Hungary

First English edition published 2012 by Telegram

1

ISBN: 978-1-84659-0948
eISBN: 978-1-84659-1235

Grateful acknowledgement to the Petőfi Literary Musem
and the Hungarian Books and Translations Office

A full CIP record for this book is available from the British Library.

A full CIP record for this book is available
from the Library of Congress.

Printed and bound by CPI Group (UK) Ltd, Croydon, CR0 4YY

TELEGRAM

26 Westbourne Grove, London W2 5RH

www.telegrambooks.com

First

The summer my father died the sun in Budapest was sweltering and oppressive. The chestnut trees along Németvölgyi Road were bowed in the extraordinary heat and the leaves of the tree in front of the house had begun to yellow much too early. Polluted air shimmered above the city. The light low-necked summer dress I had put on for the journey to the hospital seemed inappropriately coquettish in the dramatic circumstances. Neither of us knew just how dramatic at the time. On the way to the southern railway terminal, I ran past the dank-smelling cellar doors of Nagyenyed Street and stopped for a moment where the roads crossed. I looked up at the Magdalena Tower on Castle Hill; it was like a faraway, undulating mirage. The road was being mended in Alkotás Street: one section was closed off and the traffic in both directions was diverted down the lane the other side of the tramline. The throbbing machinery seemed to be swaying ominously in the heat: three iron witches stirring black soup in a cauldron. The traffic lights weren't working. As I crossed the tracks keeping an eye on traffic from the right I was almost knocked down by a car moving in the opposite direction. The car braked in time but almost broke Gigi's watch on my wrist. I started back in shock. The driver shook his fist in fury while I spread my arms in apology, as if to say I had never expected the traffic to come at me from that direction.

My father knew nothing of the heat. He was shivering in vest, pyjamas and dressing gown in the private room that Dr Cserjés, the man with the golden touch, had procured for him at the end of the corridor on the second floor of the hospital. My father sat in his narrow domain of off-white ceramic tiles, complete with metal cupboard and metal-framed chair, his iron bed squeezed between two of its walls, untouched by the heatwave that was turning the whole city into a sticky molten mass. He was preoccupied with the task of getting the manuscript of his latest book into shape. It was the second time he had found himself in hospital with a brain tumour, and the very day the children and I had arrived from Geneva. When it first happened seven years earlier Dr Cserjés operated and after the critical five years of post-surgery my father was supposedly cured. In the summer of 1999 when, to the surprise of everyone, the tumour reappeared, secretly reinstalling itself in my father's ever-active brain, the doctors decided on a second operation, my father's only regret being that this meant the loss of precious months of work on his book.

His room was on the second floor of the National Neurosurgical Institute, commonly known as the hospital in Amerikai Road. The hospital had once been a Jewish charitable institution. I have no idea whether my father knew that he had returned to the bosom of his ancestors to die or whether his iron will had wiped any reference to Judaism from his encyclopaedic mind. In the first few days, with a great deal of determination, we managed to help him downstairs to the courtyard with its stunted trees and scratched benches which was all that remained of the gardens that once surrounded the hospital. Since then movement had become so difficult for him that we no longer tried to get him into the fresh air. The next time I saw the courtyard was when my sister and I crossed it a week after the last walk, on the way to the mortuary. I was astonished to see how small the remaining island of green was among the mass of chaotically built ancillary buildings. The week before, when every step was a struggle for my father, it had seemed enormous.

In the first few days of that hot July we did not yet know that they were to be my father's last. Most afternoons, I hurried down the metro steps, slipped in through the automatic doors of the carriage, changed to the rattling little Millennial Line and, once out, ran along Hermina Street, my mind preoccupied with the problems of everyday life. There were no eloquent messages of farewell, no right to famous last words. I strode over the steaming asphalt with the blind self-confidence of the living, a mother with small children, someone replete with qualifications, quite capable of making a successful career abroad; I cut through queues smelling of perspiration, smiling at the porter whose brows wrinkled with suspicion as I passed him like someone on a special mission. The mission was to arrive at my father's bedside. I did not admit, even to myself, that this apparent self-confidence concealed the silent terror of not finding him on the ward.

When I entered the room my father was sitting on his bed fiddling with his notes and trying to consume the rest of his by-now cold dinner. His movements had slowed, his look was a touch clouded, his voice weaker and more shaky than before, but beyond that there was no sign that he was about to die. His face lit up when he saw me. He put down whatever was in his hands and looked up at me expectantly.

'What news?' he asked.

Apart from referring to the business of doctors' rounds and general hospital routine, he had nothing new to say. My mother brought him the daily papers each morning but he no longer wanted to speak about the news printed there. He listened patiently as I recounted the previous day's domestic affairs, then turned passionately to his chief concern. The most pressing of these was the manuscript in which he was trying to explain why 'really-existing socialism' – to the building of which he had given his entire life – had collapsed. Each evening I would carefully read the chapters he had finished and we'd spend the following day's visit discussing how to perfect the text. Despite the fact that it was many years since I had read anything he had written and that he had long given up the idea of discussing with me the things that were most important to him, we made allowances for each other. Perhaps this should have served as a warning that some major change was about to occur at a deep level. But we both pretended not to have heard the ominous rumblings of that change and spent our time discussing whether the third chapter should come before the second or vice versa.

It was my mother who saved my father's life while it was still possible to save it. The first time he was ill the diagnosis showed two large growths in his head: they were assumed to be of such distinct metastases that they were not worth operating on. It was at the end of a hot August and, by some quirk of fate, I had just arrived in Budapest on my way to a conference in Helsingør, Denmark. Before leaving, I spent a couple of days happily traipsing the streets of my birthplace. One afternoon, on the way home, to my greatest surprise, I came across my father on the metro. He was sitting opposite me with two enormous suitcases, one on either side of him, a red-faced, heavy-breathing fellow passenger.

'Where are you going?' I asked him, astonished.

'Home,' my father groaned.

'And the two suitcases?'

'Books. They kicked me out, you know.'

My father had been teaching a good thirty years in one of the Budapest universities. He had long passed pensionable age but would have been happy to work on had they not unexpectedly told him at the beginning of the summer that he must go. I knew this was a terrible blow for him, but he looked perfectly all right the morning he set out.

'Are you ill?' I asked.

'I have a terrible headache,' he answered.

'Have you taken anything for it?'

'Nothing works now.'

'What do you mean now? Has it been hurting long?'

'For weeks.'

We made our laborious way to the flat in Németvölgyi Road. One of the suitcases was so heavy I could hardly lift it. Fortunately my mother was home. We quickly put father to bed and were in the adjoining hall discussing what to do when my friend Tamás called unexpectedly and took us all straight down to the Kútvölgyi Street hospital. There they judged my father's condition to be so serious that they would not let him go home. Indicative of the dire condition of the Hungarian health care system, the result of the tests only became available after I returned from the conference in Helsingør.

Having received the diagnosis, my mother, sister and I sat in the hall, stiff with shock. We stared in front of us, my sister and I, shoulders hunched, stealing the odd glance at the widow-to-be. Hegel, Gegel, Babel, Bebel – my eyes ran across the familiar spines of the books. Family life at our place revolved around the hall. It was where we ate and left each other scrawled notes when we missed each other. The hall, like the rest of the flat, apart from the bathroom and kitchen, was lined with bookcases. Everything was flooded by the material evidence of my father's inexhaustible curiosity: books, mountains of books, that with the passing of decades had got out of hand. From classic works of philosophy to the series of 'Everything You Always Wanted to Know About …' handbooks; from the glories of world literature through to books about practical joinery, they had gathered here, books in all languages including those my father could not speak or read but some day hoped to learn; books of which, incredibly, he had actually read the most significant part.

As far as we could tell, the obsessive love of books had passed from father to son in my father's family, but since he himself was only capable of begetting girl children, it was to my sister and me that the virus was transmitted. According to family legend, my great-grandfather, after whom my father was named and whose Jewish name has now passed to my son, was a landowner who stuffed his country estate with books. He kept himself busy cultivating the seed crop he brought home from Palestine during the day, and read through the nights so as to cover the vacuum left by the death of his beloved wife. She had died giving birth to my twin great-uncles, Harry and Larry. The passion for second-hand bookshops was probably instilled in my father by his father, maybe still in Budapest but more likely in the Golden City of Prague, where they had been able to spend more time together than ever time before. When I learned to read I would run my fingers along the spines of books in the hall and repeat the authors' names aloud: Lenin – Lenin – Lenin; Lenin – Stalin – Engels; Hegel – Gegel – Bebel. In another room I discovered Babel, too, and liked to add his name to the list: Babel – Bebel, Hegel – Gegel; Gogol; Lukács – Machiavelli – Marx; Marx – Marx – Marx; Montesquieu – Jenő Rejtő. Books, books, books and, under their variegated covers, an ever-open, inexhaustible world of wonders.

At noon on Sunday, which was the only time the family was together, we would dine for hours in the hall, then sit round the now-bare table for more hours. My father would lean comfortably back, my mother would screw the serviettes into paper balls, and we would debate the great universal questions. The books on the shelves in the hall served as witnesses to discussions about such historical decisions as the introduction of gas heating (instead of coal) or the allocation of pocket money and, as we grew older, to ever more passionate exchanges and clashes between parents and children with increasingly divergent views of the world. But each time, in the end, we united to clear away the wreckage.

When Kútvölgyi Street hospital rang to inform us of the diagnosis, my mother must have felt her world had collapsed. Although he was in some respects her third child, my mother always looked up to my father. To the last moment of his life and in every second of his death my father was the sun in her sky, the hub of the natural order of things. He embodied for her everything that was noble and wise, qualities missing from her own childhood, qualities she never noticed in herself. We sat hunched and silent in the hall digesting the contents of the telephone conversation. I turned my eyes away from the books and feverishly tried to assess the likely effects of the diagnosis. My mother remained silent. She stared glumly ahead of her as if weighing up the balance of power. Then suddenly she declared:

'We're not going to let it happen.'

My sister and I looked at each other in surprise. My mother had, from her earliest childhood, been a thoroughgoing materialist. According to the medical diagnosis there was absolutely no chance of survival. But then she repeated it, even louder this time:

'We're not going to let it happen.'

It was as if she had declared war on death. Careful who you pick a fight with! The infallible primeval strength that had possessed my mother at critical points of her life began to flood through our own numb bodies. Soon the sense of helplessness was gone and we fell furiously to proposing plans to overcome the danger.

If fate had deposited him in the womb of some dreamy young woman in a country slightly west of here, Dr Cserjés, the man with the golden touch, would most certainly have been a well-groomed, moccasin-wearing, red-Cadillac-driving star of the medical profession, sauntering into operating theatres to execute a few delicate cranial incisions with his magic fingers before, having tired of it, pondering with leisure which exotic corner of the Earth he had not yet explored. Having been born in Hungary, however, he found himself in the neurological department of the hospital in Amerikai Road where, day after day, he was obliged to fight his way through a besieging army of anxious patients in fear of their lives, people stinking of poverty and crowding every spare inch of his consulting room. He had to fill in certificates by hand, stating how many pills he had prescribed and for what purpose, then to quarrel with his duty colleagues over where on Earth they could get sufficient numbers of sterile gowns for the medical students coming to watch him perform his operations.

The primeval strength emanating from my mother must have gripped the unsuspecting Dr Cserjés late one afternoon as he sipped his lukewarm Nescafé from a polystyrene cup and glanced at the acacia trees coming into leaf in front of the hospital. A mysterious gust of air must have touched his heart just as it was tiring of the struggle for survival. Mechanically, he took out the professor's file. The two lumps were clearly visible on the computer tomography image, the only question being where the original nodule was. It was a hopeless case. Dr Cserjés was just about to replace the images in the dossier when the brilliant afternoon sun that shone through the window clouded his gaze for an instant. In that beam of light the curious little suburban boy, eager for adventure as he had once been, leaned over his coffee-stained gown and pointed to a narrow, almost invisible line on the image suspended above the lamp.

'The North-West Passage,' the little boy whispered almost inaudibly. 'Don't you remember?'

The next morning Dr Cserjés's assistant called my mother and told her that the doctor would, after all, undertake the operation in the hope that there might be a single dumb-bell-shaped growth that had not spread. The chances of survival were twenty-five per cent. It was still better than certain death. We had won the first round.

Dr Cserjés was right. There was only a single tumour in my father's brain that, after an operation lasting several hours, he succeeded in cutting out. It is quite certain that it was Dr Cserjés who saved my father's life, or, more precisely, the little boy watching over his shoulders who would not be satisfied with halfway solutions. But Dr Cserjés had four indispensable associates. Before the operation and for months after there were four women – my mother, my sister, myself and a long-time colleague of my father's, Manyika – who tirelessly laboured at his various hospital beds. When my father first stood – what am I saying? – stood once more on the threshold of annihilation and peered in, repulsed, we formed a tight circle around him, orbiting him day and night, and fended off the death that stalked him. Out of one hospital and into an another, from side-effect to complication, we sat at his bedside, talking, listening, arranging affairs; then, when not beside him, meeting up to console, support and question each other; or when by ourselves in town calling on the very stones with which it was built, those dumb witnesses to his personal history, to help us. We could not relax for a single moment in case the Fates found an opportunity to wield their sharp scissors.

By the end of autumn I felt hollowed out like a butterfly's abandoned pupa, and returned to Geneva to reconnect what were, by now, the stray ends of my life. I was sure my father would survive. The ebony-black hair my mother had once fallen in love with had dropped out, his bear's growl of a voice had changed to an old man's falsetto, he had become deaf in one ear and lost his sense of balance, but he had survived. He hadn't changed an iota in terms of what he had constructed as the fabric of his life, and he had not lost faith for a minute. He saw both my children and, for a while, even thought of starting life anew. The following spring we sat on the shore of Lake Geneva eating the sandwiches my mother had prepared and packed for us.

Seven years later, in May, on a day of brilliant sunshine, Dr Cserjés informed my mother that the tumour had reappeared. My mother rang my sister, my sister called me, and I rang Manyika, saying: 'Please come, we are starting all over again,' and soon we were all together once more, ready for action at the doors of the hospital. What could be missing? My mother and sister brought the same conviction to this new trial of strength, not a whit less resolute than seven years before. But the bonds of comradeship were not as strong as they had been. Nor did I feel so much part of it. That is not to say we allowed my father to die. It was just that seven years before we were certain that my father would not die. Now, seven years older and wiser, I simply knew that everything was possible, even the prospect of my father dying, partly because he was mortal like the rest of us, and partly because – and it was only somewhere deep inside me that I dared even to form the thought – he had exhausted his resources.

'My only regret is that I am leaving with my luggage fully packed,' Béla Bartók is alleged to have said on his deathbed. That, perhaps, is what my father whispered to himself – although not to us because to do so might have been an admission that he would not only find himself in the surgery again but, this time, be obliged to remain there. But by now I knew that the suitcase had long been empty. Seven years ago I thought it possible that he could really start a new life, since that was what he had been talking about before the first operation, when he said he had been wrong and that he should have followed a different path, written different kinds of books and lived differently. For the first and only time in his life he admitted that he had loved his mother. 'If I manage to get out of here,' he kept saying, 'I will show you what is in the yellow suitcase.' The yellow suitcase contained his buried past.

Seven years ago I was continually praying that he would survive, that he would finally make an effort to be who he truly was. He did survive but there was no such effort. Maybe the energy required for it had been all used up in his battle for survival, when, in the months following the operation, he had to learn how to walk again, to write and to use a knife again. Perhaps, once he had been through that awkward process, it seemed easier to sink back into routine, into the open arms of habits, lies and half-truths. Perhaps the whole thing was impossible anyway because by that time who would have believed that his was a real change of direction rather than the kind of Damascene conversion the great majority of his generation had undergone so many times, whose most recent public manifestations we had watched with a shudder on television and read in the press ever since the 1989 régime change? Maybe it was simply impossible. But I don't think he even tried. He opened the yellow suitcase just once and carefully, anxiously spread the top layer of its contents before us. On the very top was his safe pass from Raoul Wallenberg, the photo showing a skeletal seventeen-year-old young man with a big nose and a warm open gaze. Next to it his parents' divorce document, his father's Budapest University record with laudatory notes from the famous physicist Lóránd Eötvös, a memorial plaque showing Comrade Lenin in profile, and his *For A Socialist Patria* medal. He studiously locked the seven locks of the case again so that it would remain undisturbed in his jungle-like study. For a while yet I continued feverishly searching out books for him, the material he required to write his new epoch-shaking work, but eventually we both lost enthusiasm and my father returned to writing political pamphlets. He was still striving to understand what had gone so irreparably wrong with communism and why. But the very premise from which he started guaranteed that he would fail to find a proper answer.

The seven years between my father's two illnesses were like a suspended judgement, the term of trial described in fairy tales. Whether the race we were running was against death or for life is hard to say. In the end the two are inextricably wound together. We were trying to squeeze the last drops out of life while all the time becoming familiar with the thought of death. 'My dear sister,' I wrote, 'I know the clock ticks for all of us. But, from now on, we can actually hear his clock ticking. At night, when we get into bed, I can think of little else, my one desire now at this of all times being to get pregnant.'

☙

The story of my father's death is interwoven with another story that is not concerned with the series of real changes in my father or in the events surrounding him. This other story is made up of memories, thoughts and emotions that followed, blended with and, in some cases, anticipated reality. This story unwound in me and did not end with my father's death, nor with his funeral, and will, it may be assumed, continue as long as I live, because when someone matters to us they remain a part of our lives even though the place they occupy is continually changing.

The first page of this other story begins with the scene that hot August afternoon when we finally succeeded in dragging the suitcases full of books home to Németvölgyi Road and my father lay down to rest in the parlour in a short-sleeved shirt with a wet handkerchief on the back of his neck. My mother and I sat behind him, horrified, on the other side of the glazed door, in the hall. My father must have felt a little better eventually because he got up and stood at the window. His powerful upper torso was caught in a halo of afternoon sunlight. He turned to move towards us when he suddenly swayed, stiff, like a statue about to topple. For a split second he seemed to hover in the air precisely like one of those bronze statues we had seen dragged down with ropes about their necks on TV; the arc of the statue's fall is always broken for a moment and a terrified murmur runs through the spectators as if they fear it might come to life suddenly and strike them down in a final act of revenge. When the statue finally hits the ground with a mighty crash the people in the crowd cry out and descend on it. They kick it, pick at it, beat it with their bare fists and sandaled feet, unleashing decades of fury. But even then, even when they are on top, they alone feel the pain of each blow.

Alarmed, we dashed into the room and succeeded in catching him before he fell against the table. In the midst of this confusion the bell shrilled: it was Tamás making an unexpected visit. That night I tossed and turned, sleepless in my bed, suspecting that something irredeemable was happening and that we could do nothing to stop it. Three days later, in Helsingør or some other northern city, I was sitting in a conference room, neatly dressed, solemnly listening to my fellow experts, but my head was an impenetrable ball of cotton wool. One afternoon I suddenly felt so ill that I had to leave the auditorium. I dragged myself towards the salvation of the hotel entrance in the low, slanting sunlight: the fierce unexpected cold seemed to slice right through me. I walked slowly and uncertainly as if the space before me had torn like cheap wrapping paper, as if a terrible depth of icy blackness lay in wait beyond the rip. If I fell into that chasm there would be no return.

☙

The summer my father died may have begun on that spring day in 1939 when his family was forced to leave the Golden City of Prague. They had moved there some years previously to escape the ever stricter anti-Jewish laws that no longer allowed my grandfather, Lajos, who was a doctor, to practise in fancy-folk-costume-wearing Hungary, his homeland. It did not matter that his Jewish ancestors had distinguished themselves in the 1848 War of Liberation, not to mention the First World War in which his father had been decorated as an officer. Lajos was a successful doctor who spoke many languages. Due to the *Numerus Clausus* laws limiting the number of Jews in education in Hungary, he had to do part of his degree in Czechoslovakia, which meant it was easy for him to get a job in Prague, at the

Switzerland-based company Wander. He loved curing people, but was particularly interested in research. Decades later my Australian relatives would shake their heads as they told me how during the summer holidays he would catch frogs on the family estate and dissect them while explaining the functions of various organs to the servants. While at Wander he worked specifically on a version of the vitamin drink Ovomaltin and, according to my father on one of his rare excursions into family history, it was on him and his little sister that Lajos experimented.

His childhood in Prague was the one truly golden era of my father's life. He managed later to wrest fragments of greater or lesser happiness from fate but all these were overcast by the shadow of what followed Prague. There, in the lulling peace of the mid-1930s, in that beautiful, dreaming city, my father could forget himself. He would ramble around the Old Town, along the banks of the Vltava, over the enchanted isle of Kampa, enjoying the complex cultures and traditions of the place, as well as the old-fashioned bourgeois democracy that, along with its concomitant sense of human dignity and self-consciousness, made Prague such a generous city. At school, children quickly outgrew cowboys and Indians and were playing at Spanish Civil War, though it was never easy to get anyone to be a Francoist. Crowning it all was the inexhaustible city library where my father spent long leisurely afternoons. Leaving the library, he would stroll home to the Mala Strana, past loud coffee houses full of people debating, past the tinkling of cups and raucous female laughter, noticing novelties in toyshop displays, cautiously slapping the blanket-covered sides of the by now ever-rarer cab-horses and dreamily watching round-backed trams as they clanged and turned at the heavily arcaded corner of the Malé Mesto. The Golden City was a pleasantly spacious place, far beyond the shady picnic areas in its outskirts. My father's family spent the summer holidays with Aunt Gigi in Dobsina, a Slovakian spa, or at the village of Třebíč, the home of the young girl in charge of the household staff; sometimes they would go for a couple of days to Nagyszőlős to play with distant cousins; occasionally Lajos's relatives from the Transylvanian town of Dés would appear and, when Grandmother felt particularly nostalgic, they visited her father's grave in Baden, near Vienna.

My father's days of happy drifting came to a jarring stop in the spring of 1939 when Europe abandoned the only free, democratic state of Eastern Europe to the burgeoning forces of fascism. On the day following the occupation of Czechoslovakia by German troops on 16 March 1939, Lajos received a directive telling him to leave the country within forty-eight hours. Europe had started closing its doors and his only option was to return to Horthy-run Hungary from where, a few years before, he and his family had escaped. My grandmother and the two small children left straight away, only Lajos remaining behind to settle matters regarding the flat and other miscellaneous things. Szera, my intelligent, well-travelled and ever cheerful grandmother, sat quietly on a worn velvet seat of the Budapest-bound train in her black-veiled hat.

'Good afternoon to you, Mr Inspector,' she greeted eagerly the garlic-and-cheap-brandy-smelling police officer who was checking their passports. My little-boy father was seized by an unfamiliar anxiety.

It remains an abiding mystery to me why Lajos did not simply gather up his family and set off west or south. He had the qualifications, the languages, the money – everything necessary to build a new life. It is of course true that in the following few years no part of Europe was exactly a holiday resort, but their chances of survival would have been greater than in Hungary where death was a certainty patiently waiting to call. Maybe it was his ties to the past, to the family and to the language that tugged at his heart, calling him back to Budapest, whose streets echoed with irredentist and anti-Semitic slogans. Perhaps it was love. Soon after they arrived home, Lajos and Szera divorced. My grandfather was quickly called up for forced labour service, Jews not being considered eligible for the army proper. A couple of months later, after two spells of that, he married a young woman who might have been a colleague of his in one or other of the hospitals that took pity on him and allowed him, secretly and unpaid, to practise his calling (that is, when he was not digging ditches for the amusement of his guards). In a photograph of Lajos that my father showed me just once, and even then only rather jealously, he stands smiling under a blossoming fruit tree, his arm round a young woman with beautiful eyes.

Two months later, during his next spell of forced labour service, they ordered his brigade to the Russian Front. In the autumn of 1943 my grandmother received an official letter in which the relevant authorities dryly informed her that my father was now a War Orphan. He was not a National Orphan, a title that would have conferred on him some faint melancholy glory and implied a certain level of financial support, but a War Orphan so that it was made entirely clear to one and all that, even in death, Grandfather, along with the more than half a million Jews who followed him, was no part of the Nation. But even before this letter my father was prepared for a new journey. At the end of summer 1940, hardly a year after returning from the Golden City, my grandmother took my father's hand and boarded a train.

'Say nothing about this to anyone,' Szera had warned him. The train journey of several hours was passed mostly in anxious silence.

'I'll be back for you soon,' my grandmother said, her voice breaking as she turned round and left the little boy in his short trousers clumsily waving after her on the courtyard of the foundling home.

As he stood there waving at the figure of his mother rapidly diminishing into the distance – she only turned back once but was so far off that her features were hardly distinguishable – it was as if my father were looking to shoo away the ill fortune hovering about his head. He took a few steps forward, then lowered his arm and held on to the wire fence surrounding the front yard. The dark form of my grandmother had long disappeared round a bend of the street. My father stared stiffly at the empty space by the house on the corner, then he slowly removed his fingers from the cold wire and pushed his continually slipping glasses back on to the bridge of his nose. He gazed around the empty yard. It was so quiet he could hear his heart beating fast. Maybe that is when something snapped in him. Maybe it was then, in the autumn of 1940, that the summer my father died really began.

In the first version of my personal history the wicked grandmother departs once and for all only to end her life in a charitable institution somewhere near Sydney some decades later, as lonely and as wretched as her faithless life deserved.

Four summers later, with modest German support and the active collaboration of the Hungarian public, all the remaining members of my father's family were herded up by the cock-feather-wearing militia – a police force to whom civil, democratic governments now tend to raise memorials – and sent off in sealed cattle-trucks towards the gas chambers of Auschwitz. Rich and poor, realists and dreamers, the miserly and the generous, bigots and freethinkers, women, old people, children, everyone disappeared behind the doors of the showers. But my father was beyond such concerns by then, having found his true place in a new family, the illegal Communist Party. It was I who felt the full strength of that blow forty years later when, pressed against the cold walls of the black labyrinth of Yad Vashem in Jerusalem, in every recited name I thought to recognise the names of family members long gone up in smoke.

What made my grandfather, Lajos, return home to Hungary in 1939? What made the writer György Bálint return from England, where refuge was assured, so that he would perish in the Jewish Hospital in the Ukraine two years later? Why did Walter Benjamin ignore the urgings of his friends and leave escape to the very last minute when the only way out led to pills of arsenic at Port Bau? Why did Lev Nussimbaum hang around in Rome, Vienna and Berlin, unable to believe his eyes, only to perish in Italy before he could be reduced to a mere number in one or other concentration camp?

Disbelief is the recurring motif in every survivor's story. 'I did not believe that it could happen to us, not here, not even when it was happening right in front of our eyes.' Beyond ties of affection and the desire to cling to the familiar, it is perhaps this trust that is the most important factor in explaining why six million Jews allowed themselves to be packed into wagons. Their conviction that the world was a rational place based on certain shared values was so firm that they doubted the evidence of their own senses. They simply couldn't believe they were seeing the destruction of a moral order based on the values of the Enlightenment, an order whose toppling would bury them, too.

Had my father's parents been more opportunist, had they stayed together, bound by strong ties of custom and desire for security like everyone else, they would surely have sent their children to relatives in the country in order to save them from deportation. Had they done so, the local authorities would gladly have assisted the children to clamber into the wagons in the direction of a hastily cleaned gas chamber. Perhaps they would have arrived there in the same transport as my mother's little friends, the twin girls who might still have remembered the pain and affection on my mother's face, who had wanted to say farewell to them, in one of the few gestures of empathy that might have comforted them briefly in their disgrace before they were butchered. But one of my father's parents had long vanished into dust on the wide cornfields of the Eastern Front, 'On the banks of a cool fast-flowing stream', as the popular Russian song has it, while the other, my grandmother Szera, was hiding out alone somewhere in Budapest.

My father's parents might perhaps have escaped had they not been such incorrigible dreamers. Had Lajos not always been on the look-out for something better, something more perfect, the family might have remained together in some place of refuge. Then the divorce that was bound to follow would have been a private matter, not history of the tragic kind. My father would have become a respectable bookworm, my aunt a recognised fashion designer in one of the quieter nooks of the world, and my sister and I would have remained lost opportunities in the rich storehouse of life. If Szera's survival instinct had not overcome her trust in the world order she could not have saved my father. But, on the other hand, if she had not been an incorrigible dreamer she would not have survived all that happened to her.

Szera loved Lajos, as she did his miniature mortal version, my father, with every fibre of her being. Lajos may have left her for another woman but Szera was convinced that once the bad times were over he would come to his senses and return to his family. This blind and tempting hope was ended by the receipt of the curt message that Lajos had perished somewhere in the Ukraine. Szera was without money or work, alone in Budapest – a city that had turned into a deathtrap – with two small children. Her family had been scattered, her friends were either in hiding, or deported, or had already leapt through windows to their deaths. In the early autumn of 1940 my grandmother took the desperate step of placing her son in an orphanage and her daughter in a Catholic convent, so that there should be not the least shadow of doubt that they were not Jewish. A couple of years later, when my father was expelled from the foundling home and returned to Budapest, his mother was living in a sublet in Bródy Sándor Street, where he sheltered until he found a reasonably well-paid position as a delivery boy at a second-hand bookstore. In the bloody months of 1944, Szera, who allegedly had some kind of direct line to the Swedish Embassy and its life-saving staff, got him a specially manufactured Swedish passport, one of Raoul Wallenberg's *Schutzpasses*. When my father demanded more, Grandmother managed to procure enough documents to supply the needs of the whole underground communist cell.

After the war, while her son was preoccupied with the task of saving the world and her daughter was falling resoundingly in love, Szera, left alone, tried to steady her boat on the extraordinarily troubled waters of politics in the new People's Democracy. She understood nothing, nor was there anyone in a position to explain things to her. Her nearest relatives, together with their families, had either been killed in the war or were adrift in the world somewhere inside or beyond the borders. Szera was hoping her darling firstborn would appear and enlighten her. The darling firstborn, however, was involved in preparations for the 1948 elections on behalf of the Communist Party. Like many other women of her class, Szera had no education or work experience that might have offered her the means to a livelihood. She survived by trading money on the black market, the money sent by her brother Izidor, a gentleman of substantial means who looked like Paul Newman and who had had the historical foresight to move to Australia before the war. The Hungarian forint was weakening all the time so this was likely to have been a remunerative activity and the vigilant authorities quickly spotted what she was doing and threw her into prison along with other speculators. Szera waited in vain for her son to arrive like a prince on a white charger to rescue her. When the appointed comrades investigated his background and found that he was the son of a well-to-do Jewish family, he had to state in writing that he had cut all contact with his class-alien family. And, being a man of his word, he tried to keep this promise throughout his life.

Once Szera was set free, those few remaining members of the family who, after a long and convoluted process, finished up in Australia decided the situation was intolerable and sent her a ticket for the voyage out. My grandmother left on the last train before the Iron Curtain fell in 1948. She waited for her much-loved son to turn up so that they could board the ship together. But there was no opportunity even for a goodbye kiss. After wrestling with his conscience, my father recognised, not without a sense of relief, that her departure meant one less problem for him to deal with. If his conscience troubled him it was only on the rare occasions that his, by now very remote, mother wrote to him. I can't tell how he would have felt in 1957 when, through mysterious channels, he received an anxious letter from Szera. My grandmother wanted to know whether everyone was still alive as she had heard that there was shooting in the streets of Budapest again and she wondered about sending warm clothes for his infant children. According to family accounts he answered informal manner. 'My dear Mother,' he might have written, 'there are no shortages here, we lack nothing. We are building a new People's Democracy that has enabled me to complete my studies. I have become a doctor, like my father. I will be curing not sick individuals but sick societies.' As far as I know that was the last time they exchanged letters. As his books started to appear he would send a complimentary copy to Australia without any particular comment. Then this too stopped.

Szera's entire being was torn between the undying and, later, unrequited love of two men. She depended on them for her very existence: they inhabited every fibre of her being and ruled each beat of her heart. My grandfather was one of the two, a talented, deeply learned man who was born to be free but who was beaten or shot to death and shoved into a mass grave by a soldier who was only carrying out orders: where, when and how we shall probably never discover. The other was my father, just as talented and learned, just as liberty-seeking, who, having failed to thank her for offering him the chance of life, indeed more than once – that's what a mother is for, after all, to give life – decided to have nothing more to do with her.

Szera died in Sydney in a charitable foundation where the relatives had placed her because she was no longer capable of distinguishing reality from imagination, as they tactfully explained to me decades later. On her last bedside shelf lay a row of books by my father on the ways of perfecting 'really-existing socialism', a set of texts that remained completely incomprehensible to her. An old photograph was propped against the books. It showed Lajos and Szera on the voyage home from Palestine sometime near the end of the 1920s. Despite the urgings of my great-grandfather, they did not emigrate because, emotionally, they could not bear the loss of their homeland. There they are, standing arm-in-arm on the deck of a ship. They are holding their faces up to the fresh sea breeze. Szera wears a beatific smile. She has not yet told anyone that she is returning home, her womb heavy with secret fruit.

ଓ

Barely a generation after my family hurriedly left the Golden City behind, near the end of the period of winter examinations, I set out in high spirits to visit Prague with a bunch of friends. The city was grey, melancholy and hostile. After sunset we were ambling down a street near the unlit Gunpowder Tower. Pedestrians scattered in panic when we approached them for directions. At the inns they glared at us in an unfriendly manner any time we burst into loud laughter. The cold had penetrated to my bones but I could not help but be touched by the beauty of the place.

'Just imagine, they refused to speak to us merely because we were Hungarians!' I complained to my father once we got home.

My father kept a dark silence. 'Traitors,' he muttered to himself.

I didn't know what he was talking about but felt sad that the Eden of his childhood should have been ruined in such a mean way. I had no idea then how it was that our brotherly army had marched into the Golden City to drown in blood the last great experiment in socialism with a human face. What might my father have felt on seeing tanks rolling through the streets of Prague again? What did he think when he read, in confidential files reserved only for trusted cadres, of the self-immolation of Jan Palach and others, of street signs deliberately reversed, of dismantled machinery in the factories, of the signs of open opposition among the masses? Could he have been left entirely cold by the despair of all those who had believed that the system could be improved from within but then saw that hope crushed by tanks in a process apparently so natural it seemed the only possible way of proceeding?

I only learned about what really happened in Czechoslovakia in 1968 much later from a Greek friend. In the years of the gradual relaxation of really-existing socialism we were permitted to make an excursion to the West every third year. Once there, this young Greek spent his bitterly hoarded hard currency, not on jeans, hot-dogs and pornographic films like the decisive majority of our countrymen in the lands of the free, but on reading right through the documents of the Prague Spring of 1968 in a library in Paris. On his return to Budapest, genuinely shocked, he revealed his findings to a startled group of friends. That large group, of which I was one, was chiefly composed of the children of people who belonged to the communist movement and whose inherited faith in the resounding rightness of the system was confirmed by the testimonies of Chilean, Greek and Algerian refugees. All I remember is the silence that followed the young Greek's account. My God, I thought, if this is all true we really are in trouble.

But of course it couldn't be true.

ᏫᏋ

The summer my father died might just as likely have begun the summer he reached the age at which his own father had been killed. This death, that he could not imagine, that was not marked with a grave, must have hung over my father's head like a dark cloud until he reached the age of forty-three. Perhaps it was only then that he embarked on his own mortality. But that dark cloud had settled in his heart. In 1968 he contracted pneumonia and after that we were always worried about his heart. Thirty years later, when the second brain tumour was operated on and my sister and I hurried into the hospital, the doctor's first question was about the condition of his heart. Had he had problems? I ask you! Who in this country does not have heart problems?

ᏫᏋ

It was Attila József who got my father expelled from the orphans' home. By the time he was fifteen, my father was a committed young communist who could immediately trace the cause of every ill back to the issue of class struggle. At the year-end celebration of the institution, when all obedient little orphans licked their hair into shape and joined in a ceremony to express their gratitude for the generosity of their keepers, my father stood at the centre of the podium in his short pants, his legs like pipe-stems, nervously adjusted his wire-framed glasses and, instead of delivering the lyrical passage he had learned by heart, he recited Attila József's ballade which has the repeated end line 'The profit goes to the capitalist'. By the third time he had repeated that line, pointing with grand gestures at the assembled philanthropic ladies and pince-nez-wearing gentlemen, they had recovered from the shock and given voice to their indignation. He never got as far as the *envoi*. They expelled him there and then. He travelled to Budapest and found work on some factory floor, then later as a bookshop delivery boy, earning his pittance that way while spreading the Word among the poor and downtrodden.

My father was standing in the crowded storeroom of the boulevard bookshop where he worked waiting for the manager to pack an outgoing parcel. He took a deep breath of the freshly printed and old books, relishing their characteristic smells – that long-lasting memory of the union of ink and paper – and loitered in the badly lit space, feeling there was nothing he desired more than to remain there in its benevolent half-light and silence. He stumbled about by the light of the bare bulb and hungrily surveyed books stacked on shelves to the ceiling, books he only dared approach when the manager and his older assistant were out in the shop with a more important customer. He breathed in the homely book smell and suddenly in the dim light he felt a hand on his shoulder. The light but firm touch on his narrow shoulders was so familiar that a sharp mixture of happiness and grief flashed through him. He gave a mighty sigh.

'Don't worry, son. Sit down and read until I'm ready.' The old man looked up at him from behind his glasses.

'Thank you,' my father mumbled.

Then he grabbed the nearest book and quickly sat down as if to cram back into his narrow frame the rush of desire that wanted to explode within him. Once the manager had finished packing the parcel, my father stuck it under his arm and stepped out into busy Múzeum Boulevard. He saw with delight that his fellow delivery boy, Gyuri Sándor, was also ready to set off. They were like brothers, two thin, bespectacled, orphaned Jewish boys who had found temporary shelter in the intimate cavern of the bookshop. They blended with the loud traffic of the boulevard and, oblivious to everything else, debated the politics of the Social Democratic Party.

Gyuri who, thanks to great good fortune, like my father had survived both the war and the 1950s, was his best friend. It is true that later, in the 1960s, my father was constantly upbraiding him, even in personal letters, because he spent too much time on the mysteries of finance when he should have been building socialism with the Party, but Gyuri was the only person, other than my mother, with whom my father could relax a little without feeling obliged – even while sipping at his coffee after Sunday lunch – to be fighting his corner for the Cause. In 1944 they rented a servants' room facing the air shaft or *lichthof* that served to ventilate the service rooms of the elegant tenement buildings opposite. The room's one window opened on to the window of a wealthy middle-class family's pantry. The two constantly hungry boys would open the window in the evening and enjoy the spiced sausage smell as it wafted across the stinking shaft. One evening the window opposite was left open. The two stood bright-eyed on their creaky stool and counted the revealed blessings of Canaan before them.

'Sixteen sticks of sausage, six cuts of ham and ten sides of bacon,' my father announced, his voice trembling.

'Look at the smaller piece, there on the right. They've eaten some of it already!' Gyuri whispered excitedly. 'Let's push that plank of wood across and I'll climb over and slice off a piece. They'll never even notice!'

'Are you mad!' my father answered, though in his mind he was measuring the length of plank they used as a table and wondering if it would reach. They lived on the fifth floor.

'No problem, you'll see! We'll just take a couple of centimetres. Where's your penknife?'

'Absolutely not!' my father replied with sudden resolve. The champion of truth overcame the hungry child in him.

'Come on, just five centimetres,' Gyuri begged. 'They're bourgeois in any case. They deserve it.'

'Yes, they deserve it, but that is not the way to deal with the bourgeoisie,' my father declared. Now that he had found the right verbal formula it was easier to suppress the rumblings of his stomach. 'Honest people do not steal. We can only triumph over them if everything we do sets an example to the masses.'

'What masses?' asked Gyuri, exasperated.

But he knew the game was up. They closed the window and went out for a walk so they wouldn't have to think about what lay behind it. After that my father maintained that the window should not be opened in case they were weakened by vain fantasies. A couple of weeks later Ferenc Szálasi, leader of the fascist Arrow Cross, took over the running of the country and made quite sure that there would be no fantasising of any sort, not even by accident.

My father remained scrupulously honest all his life. He never cheated or stole, never submitted to corruption and had no yearning for any kind of material reward. This sense of utter irreproachability, to which I bore daily witness, was one reason why I never suspected the kind of distortions and suppressions of truth that lay deep below the surface.

☙

It is possible that the summer my father died started at the beginning of the summer of 1972 after all, on that pleasantly warm afternoon when a well-dressed stranger rang the door bell of our flat in Németvölgyi Road. My sister opened the window. The man behind the metal grille was looking for my father.

'My father isn't at home,' my sister said and was about to close the window.

'I bring news about your grandmother,' said the man.

My sister gazed at him in wonder. What kind of news could this dandified figure be bringing us about our black-headscarved grandmother?

'Your Australian grandmother,' the dandy added quickly when he noticed the astonishment in those beautiful feline eyes.

'I don't have an Australian grandmother,' my sister replied dryly and slammed down the window.

She went back into the hall, picked up the book lying on the table and the remains of her ham roll, and immersed herself in her reading again. After a short while the bell rang again. My sister jerked her head back in annoyance and saw through the glazed entrance door that the stranger was still there. This was just too much.

'What do you want?' she shouted. 'I don't have an Australian grandmother and I don't need any car insurance.'

'Your aunt, Erika Holló, sent me from Australia,' the man shouted back with a touch of despair in his voice.

My sister felt uncertain for a moment. The name was familiar. Every time we filled in an official document we had to declare whether any of our family was resident abroad. This was the name we always had to put down, but whenever we asked our father who she was he replied it was his sister but that he had no idea whether she was dead or alive.

'Then why do we have to put her name down?' we asked in puzzlement. 'She's not a real relative then.'

'We have to put it down because it is the truth and if we kept quiet about it there could be trouble,' came the answer. This was undoubtedly convincing. You can't suppress the truth, not even when it is unpleasant.

'The one who left the country with a legal passport and official permission?' my sister enquired from the hall.

The man standing by the door couldn't have understood this properly but was immediately aware of the doubt that had entered my sister's voice.

'Yes, yes, that's it exactly!' he bellowed heartily.

And that is how Árpi gained entrance to the hall of our flat in Németvölgyi Road. After a while my mother and I appeared and listened in astonishment as he told his story. He himself was a refugee from 1956, a friend and business partner of my father's sister in a children's boutique in Sydney. He was visiting home on family and business matters and was taking the opportunity to look us up on our aunt's behalf. My grandmother Szera had finally died of old age at the beginning of the summer. Since she had continually spoken of my father before her death they felt it was important to let us know.

That day my father came home unexpectedly early. The trade union was planning the next end-of-year festivities so everyone had stopped work. His years in the Soviet Union had taught him the vital importance of alcohol in developing human relationships and he was capable of putting down a respectable amount of liquor without the least sign of drunkenness. But now, on this mild early summer evening when we were almost sick with anticipation waiting for him to come home, he returned in a mildly drunken state. There was a faint sour cabbage smell on his breath, too, as if he were a genuine rake. He clattered through the door, his sparkling black eyes blinking at us with satisfaction, taking not the blindest bit of notice of the desperate glances exchanged between my mother and me. My sister had vanished into thin air. My father took a long time washing his hands, put on his slippers and reclined complacently in the armchair, waiting for my mother to serve up his supper. After supper my mother told him about the visitor. A shadow passed across my father's face. There was no change in his expression, but the glow of satisfaction immediately disappeared. He silently toyed with the forks left on the table, clearing his throat from time to time. He lingered in the hall for a while then retired to his study. My mother followed him shortly afterwards while I escaped into the children's room.

☙

My father's life was conducted in two places. He thought, read, made notes, wrote and slept in his study at home. Nor was his office at the university exclusively for working: it was where he met his comrades, his students and his colleagues; it was where he conducted exams with his students ; where he listened to the complaints of those who needed help and where he handed out good advice late into the night. We often joked that he should have been priest at a confessional or a psychologist rather than an academic; the long queue at his office door comprised those who wanted either professional advice, political direction or consolation. Teaching did not end for him with the delivery of his material and the supervision of his students' work; the university was an inexhaustible goldmine where he could exercise his philanthropic instincts and set doubting souls on the right road. The right road, naturally, was the road to socialism, the building of which required absolute dedication and – when need be – a dose of constructive criticism. One could only judge the system from the inside, of course, because outside criticism weakened and undermined it: even constructive criticism from within was to be tolerated only from those who accepted the fundamental principles of the movement, such as the leading role of the Party and the overarching dogma of socialist ownership.

My father's two places of work were more or less identical twins. Both were crammed with piles of books, notes, works of scholarship, newspapers. Sometimes the situation became so acute that there was only enough space on his desk for a sheet of paper. Those surfaces the word did not completely cover were stuffed with souvenirs of travels, and small, mostly tasteless gifts from people who either admired or were obliged to him, though there were one or two real treasures among them: an African mask, a genuine Russian samovar, and the Arab language theoretical review of the clandestine Iraqi Communist Party. Hidden among the books and various knick-knacks there were miscellaneous items that 'would come in useful some time', anything from a set of drill heads to an electric water heater. The two rooms were connected in one direction by a rumbling tramline and, very often, by a cheap and reliable taxi service that could be hailed quite easily on the corner of Böszörményi Street. It was often needed because my father was constantly running out of time and was always late. The other way, at night, it came down to a solitary walk. We were familiar, though even then only to a minor degree, with the empire at home, since we would often sneak in there and look for clues when my father was away. But not even my mother laid foot in the university office, or only very occasionally.

Anything that happened outside these rooms was of secondary importance to my father. Even though the whole of family life revolved around him, at home he was like some high-ranking, if rather preoccupied, visitor who was pleased enough to spend some time chatting with his hosts, discovering what they were thinking, but then excused himself because urgent matters of the utmost importance required his attention.

My sister and I suspected that his mysterious, impenetrable study was the true home of the Cause, the Cause being the faceless, secretive, never-to-be-satisfied stranger with whom my father spent the greatest part of his time. In so far as our childish imaginations could determine, this Cause came clothed in petitions, manifestos, notes and ordinances, as well as in long analytical essays, in meetings that lasted whole nights and were conducted in interminable, endless whispers. The Cause was there in everything my father did. It was in what he wrote, in what he read, in what he said, in what he dreamed, in how he argued, told stories and harangued; it was in the way he prepared articles or proposals. The latter were addressed to those who were even more dutiful servants of the Cause than he could ever be, people who were in a position to act on his farsighted proposals much more effectively than, as he would say, an anonymous unimportant person like him, a mere teacher at the university. One could sense a certain underlying bitterness in his way of formulating this that made us suspect that our father was not altogether happy. He consecrated all his life and efforts to the Cause, but still he did not have the self-assuredness of the insiders. He did all he could to demonstrate his loyalty to the Cause but, as far as we could tell, they let him know regularly enough that he was merely a tolerated outsider whose services they might call on as and when the mighty engine of power that worked in mysterious ways and according to an impenetrable logic so required, but that he personally was of no account.

I don't know when the appetite for truth was supplanted in my father's heart by the notion of unconditional service to the Cause. Perhaps it was at that first election with the blue ballot papers; perhaps it was when he, the grandson of landed Jews, had to face the disillusioned peasantry during the forced collectivisation campaign. It might have been when the Party disciplined him on account of his untrustworthy family background and when he understood that his survival would not be guaranteed in his new, personally chosen family either; when he realised that not only those to whom he was tied through the blind, uncontrollable attachments of blood but those to whom he was joined on the basis of ideological conviction could turn against him at any time. Decades later, during the series of complications that followed the first operation when he was shifted from hospital to hospital and when I traipsed the town trying to get him an exemption, I was unable to catch the moment when the serenity and trust that could be seen in his eyes, even on the *Schutzpass*, was extinguished, when the gaze of the seeker after truth was replaced by the look of knowledge of undisputed truth. From that time on in his life the Cause provided the right perspective on everything from classic literature through to ice-skating, from the education of his children through to weekend leisure activities. There was no point in us weeping over the fate of Dostoevsky's Prince Mishkin, since Mishkin was a hopeless idealist, the pipedream of some retrograde element. On the other hand, we were obliged to take to heart the Protopopovs, the Olympic gold medallist figure-skating couple, because they demonstrated the superiority of the Soviet system. But at least we got to know both.

Second

My father's days in hospital were efficiently planned. In the early morning my mother would visit, equipped with clean pyjamas, a towel, some food and the newspapers, taking care of his physical needs. After that she would yield her place to the girls, that is to say my elder sister, myself and Manyika. Manyika was a beady-eyed widow of indeterminate age who was at one time an assistant secretary at the university and who faithfully followed my father into communism's ever more obscure corners. My mother kept visitors strictly at bay so we were a little surprised when Manyika first appeared on the ward. But my father looked pleased: it seemed that even in hospital he welcomed the unconditional hero-worship radiating from those chicken-like eyes, not to mention the accounts of goings-on at the latest Party meeting. Manyika became a regular visitor by stealth, without anyone objecting. From time to time I tried to engage her in conversation but I couldn't make head or tail of her confused monologues. My father's most faithful disciple, I once remarked, but my mother quickly put me right on that. After the funeral we never saw her again, though for years afterwards we kept finding withered red carnations on his grave. There must have been others like Manyika who regarded him as 'one of their own deceased'.

My mother would return to the hospital in the afternoon to help my father bathe because he found it ever harder to move. My shift was the late afternoons when my mother or sister could look after the children. In the evenings, when I wasn't meeting some particularly close friend, which, in those first few days, was rather frequently, I'd be grinding my teeth, reading over my father's manuscripts so that we could continue work the next day. Not even my anxiety about his condition could relieve the sense of despair I felt reading his words. It seemed it wasn't just physical sickness that was seizing hold of him. It was as if he had already set out on his final journey back in time and got stuck in the early 1950s, his writing having ossified into a testament characteristic of those times. There was no sign in his manuscript that anything had changed in the last forty years, nothing of the tragic yet instructive lessons he was forced to learn that made him shift from a stout dogmatic to a dogmatic ready to compromise. It was as if even here, in the work that was to be his summa, his bequest to the world, he was missing the point, omitting what was most essential, as if – and I shuddered at the thought – he had completely missed out on his own life.

And of course, once a thought like that enters a person's head, it is impossible not to ask what is essential. Honest self-examination is at the heart of it. The admission of some truth. The debt we must pay – as the Cseh Tamás song has it – to our venerable Great Uncle Reality, a figure my father refused to recognise, much as he did with his twin uncles, Harry and Larry, long thought dead, who suddenly turned up in Budapest in the mid-1970s, just as our country was moving to the gentler slopes of goulash communism. My father's spiritual bequest was not the honest account of a wise survivor: it was not his life and historical experience, but a word-for-word rehash of classic Marxist precepts. Given his situation, it was impossible to argue this with him, so at night on top of the trouble of grinding my teeth reading his manuscript, I had to invent intellectual acrobatics to formulate my views in a gentle way for the following day. 'What kind and lovely words can I greet him with?'

It might be that my father returned to the direct quotation of long moribund texts because he had a lifelong religious reverence for words. It was the point at which Jewish and communist habits of mind met in him. Facts and empirical evidence were mere data: what mattered was the Word uttered by the heroic champions of truth. Marx was, no doubt, a rare genius, someone who could see below surface trivialities to underlying systems, and even got to name them, but those who trod in his giant footsteps and called themselves his followers had no such ambitions. What they lost in following him was the very essence of his work: that unsparing, razor-sharp critique of both the world and himself. The struggle against the narrow possession and monopolisation of power was replaced by the exercise of a power more comprehensive and absolute than any before. To cover this, meaningless slogans were repeated *ad infinitum*, offering an ever more dilute sense of purpose that some time later could be easily converted to the equally hollow, equally false slogans of consumerism promising instant happiness to people accustomed to being guided like sheep.

The desire for an ideal society, one that would finally abolish the poverty and injustice that had been an inevitable part of our history, was always in my father's thoughts. It offered a collective solution and those who shared it were not afraid to declare that man could not be happy alone. Even the most passionate of lovers would find their love poisoned if their paths were constantly beset by begging children and rough-sleeping tramps. Of course, sooner or later my father had to notice that the gap between reality and desire was growing ever wider and more frightening. Since reality could not be winched up to the level of desire, he was obliged to drag desire down to the filthy soil of reality. Naturally, this meant terminally downgrading the ideal, but there was no way back; every last ounce of creative effort was required to argue that the unattractive aspects of the system happened to be incidental and that the Party leadership – with the help of its allies – would quickly put those right.

I myself had inherited that unfailing belief in spoken or written words, but a few dramatic encounters with reality had shaken it. It took me a long time to realise that words were not only an irresistible source of revolutionary energy that could pass through barbed wire, iron curtains and concrete walls and uncover truths that had been suppressed, but that they could also be miserable, meaningless drudges employed to hide the truth. But in the first throes of my idealism, the word was sacred. Until I was thirteen and first saw the sea, I would spend long afternoons checking adult claims to the effect that 'The sea is infinite!' against elementary school maps that showed clearly demarcated pools of blue.

> *From the Archive of Unsent Letters and Unspoken Words:*
> Highly Esteemed Cartographer Kogutowitz Manó, who designed all maps hanging on the walls of our schools! Who is right?

'Leave while you can,' a wise and sensitive young worker told me at the steelworks in Csepel, the working-class borough of Budapest, where I was spending my school holiday so I could experience Reality at first hand while earning some money for a trip at the end of the summer.

'I'm only here in the holidays,' I answered as if by way of excuse while we pushed the steel rods through into the noisy workshop.

'That's all right then,' he replied glumly. 'You're lucky,' he added and kept his mouth shut after that, even through the ten-minute cigarette break.

We sat opposite each other in silence on the long wooden benches of the smoking room. He blew out smoke and gazed thoughtfully at his boots. What did he mean? My own experience confirmed that eight hours of exhausting work as well as the hours of necessary travelling before and after were not terribly conducive to pondering mankind's salvation: the first thing was to get to bed as quickly as possible. I certainly never once heard my tired, ill-tempered, boiler-suited fellow workers debating the great issues of life. Conversation was restricted to everyday frustrations, the difficulties of making a living, and the doings of management. Might it be that the working class had not inherited the earth? But who had inherited it then? Surely not I, I who rushed from our book-lined flat down the chestnut-lined avenues of Buda every morning to catch the 6:30 local train to Csepel? Or was it my father? But my father was penniless. He lived in a rented apartment, without a car, without a holiday house, apparently with no personal needs, a man in a cheap suit with bulging pockets whose every evening and most weekends were dedicated to the Cause. My father, Comrade Fülöp Holló, didn't count. But then who did?

This wasn't a question I could ask, not even of Cartographer Kogutowitz Manó.

Decades later, when I read the British historian Bill Lomax's book and the memoirs of István Eörsi about the workers' organisations of 1956, works that had been carefully kept from the public eye, I began to understand the note of bleak resignation in my boiler-suited colleague. But back then in the 1970s and 1980s, in the course of my various summer jobs, sheer stupidity or innocence protected me and I couldn't understand why the leading class, the vanguard of the revolution, was so miserable.

'Look, Fülöp, the working class doesn't believe it's in

charge!' I dared announce one evening while tending to my blistered hands.

'They'll learn,' my father answered with his usual self-assurance. 'They don't know it, but they are,' he continued before going on to a passionate exposition of Hegel and the role of unconscious forces in the historical process.

My father had a reassuring answer for everything. He never left matters in the air with a careless half-finished sentence but explained things seriously and thoroughly. Any time my faith in a better future wavered, any time I felt some people were not giving their all in the struggle to liberate mankind, not even the official representatives of the system, he assured me my fears were groundless. There was always an explanation ready to hand and the explanation was always convincing. That is, until the facts that I was obliged to face ever more frequently as time went by grew more persuasive than his arguments.

All the same, I held firm for a long time. My faith in my father was not shaken too much even in the maelstrom of adolescence. It was the early 1970s and there were certain stirrings in the country that remained invisible to me, but I sensed them with a mixture of anxiety and curiosity. Everything seemed more complicated, more provisional. I began to see that my teachers might not be infallible, that the textbooks tended to present a watered-down version of the truth, so one was always forced to go back to a primary source and that those excerpts from poems highlighted in bold type in our classrooms always lacked something, something that would utterly transform their meaning. I understood that not everyone believed what we did, and that those who thought differently were not necessarily monsters.

My best friend of the time was István, a boy a couple of years older than me, who painted abstract pictures and read books by authors largely unknown to me. We'd argue through the night, watch movies with a ferocious thirst and laugh a great deal about the idiocies of the adult world. Some years later it became pointless beating at his door: he was either in bed, drunk or wandering the streets somewhere. But in 1972 all life lay before us. One bright morning we skipped school and sat on a park bench behind Fisherman's Bastion up in the Castle district of Budapest, soaking in the sun. The busy city throbbed beneath our feet like a wonderful, regular heart. Above us time stood still. We didn't know much about the world, but were properly touched by its grandeur.

'Did you know your father is a bastard?' my friend asked suddenly. No, I didn't know. And nor did I want to know.

'No need to be so shocked,' István laughed as he looked at me. 'He'll get off his pedestal sooner or later. Come on, let's see the archaeological dig.'

The well-known archaeologist László Zolnay and his team had just unearthed marble statues from the time of King Sigismund, in a ditch first dug over five hundred years ago. We had marvelled at these unexpected messengers of the past at a hastily arranged exhibition and had often called in to see how the archaeologists at the bomb-shattered Sándor Palace near by were doing. Perhaps the soil beneath us had more to offer. We stood around watching them like supporters at a football match. These were the advantages of living behind the Iron Curtain. The Castle district was ours. Our favourite adolescent gathering places were the Tárnok café and The Black Raven restaurant. The past hadn't yet been offered to tourists prepared to pay for it. It belonged to us, maybe because we were labouring under the misapprehension that the future was also ours.

❧

When my father wasn't shuttling between his two offices, when he was neither teaching nor in meetings, he'd drift about the city. Walking was an essential activity for him, as it had been for his father, as vital as his passion for thoroughness and books. The reason he had to walk in the city, he told us, was because it was his way of switching off: he looked in every shop window, read every poster and, naturally, called in at every second-hand bookshop. The only thing that could drag him from his two offices was the prospect of travel. He was a great traveller. Wherever he found himself, within moments he could locate his position and begin to understand the language; he would immediately familiarise himself with the local transport system and know where to seek out the best-hidden treasures of the place. He'd collect the publicity leaflets, the newspapers he found on park benches and on the train, the various guides and maps, and would spend the evenings working his way through vast piles of paper to acquaint himself with the territory opening up around him.

This impressive knack of landing on his feet was certainly an aspect of his secret genetic inheritance. The experience of those generations before him of being constantly on the run had worked its way into his very cells: shifting landscapes were second nature to him. The scenes of his childhood were dispersed among East Central Europe's then still comfortable nooks and crannies and he moved between them with ease. But this ready and natural sense of mobility came to a sudden end in his adult life. The borders were concreted over and fenced in with barbed wire. Crossing one, even between comrade countries, became a frightening procedure that could take hours, entailing a baggage search at every station manned by armed guards, in the course of which every compartment, every seat and every luggage rack was thoroughly examined, while the guards frowned on people as though everyone had something to hide and it was only because of their generosity that they let us get away with it – this time. My parents behaved as though this was the most natural thing in the world.

But my father's restlessness would not let him be and, whenever he could, he set out on a journey. His professional trips were for decades restricted to the countries of the Eastern Bloc. He was like a caged animal. He seemed to know by heart the timetables of all the Polish, Bulgarian and East German railways, to say nothing of the outstanding monuments of Our Great Soviet Homeland, and then, finally, in the mid-1970s he was allowed to explore the sinful West. This was, of course, only so that he could unmask it all the better. My parents embarked on this journey happily, my mother bringing enough supplies for weeks of travel, while my father had two enormous briefcases stuffed full of books, notes and the obligatory bottle of Ararat cognac.

All roads led to the city for my father. There was never any time in the programme for trips to the countryside. Unlike other members of the workers' movement, who enjoyed country walks, singing and popular culture, for him nature was first and foremost an obstacle to be overcome. The role of the crowning triumph of nature (*Homo socialisticus*) was to rein in nature, and with a loud flourish of trumpets to conduct it into a life of noble servitude. The point of the flourish, of course, was to blot out the ancient caveman's dread of forces that could not be controlled, though, understandably enough, these were not matters that tended to preoccupy the apostles of scientific socialism. In cities it is easier to maintain the illusion that our business is with a world we ourselves have created and can control. It is no accident that the most crackpot dictators of the twentieth century, from Mussolini through to Ceauşescu, wanted to turn their lovely cities into vulgar images of themselves. My father felt much safer in a city than among mountains or by an unpeopled seashore. In foreign cities he relaxed, strangely enough, and allowed himself to be led by their tides. It was as if the impressionable young boy who could never get enough of the world had taken over from the disciplined, stern adult.

The first trip abroad my parents took us on was to the capital of East Germany, Berlin. For a child like me who had grown up under the spell of concrete borders it was a memorable occasion. The night before we set off I was so excited my mother had a hard job getting me to bed. At dawn I dreamed that the world beyond our borders was exactly the same as ours: grass was green, sky was blue and roofs were red. The next day when, hearts wildly beating, we eventually succeeded in crossing the border, I kept quiet about my disappointment in finding that my dream was true. Apart from this, Berlin served up plenty of nice surprises. The city was ringed by roads with buildings made of concrete blocks and great linked lakes that you could row around. The most impressive sign of technological advance, like a modest herald of the promised socialist paradise, was the escalator, the moving stairs in one of the department stores. I spent hours riding up and down it, dazzled by the brilliant new dawn it promised.

The apartment in which my parents' friends lived was of spotless Spartan rigour and demanded impeccable behaviour on our part. The tablecloth was at perfect right angles to the table and Auntie Gerda set the table with silver cutlery including a special knife for fruit. The only time I had seen such tableware was in the grandiose salons of Festetich Palace in Keszthely.

'Are they nobility, Mother?' I asked anxiously one night when we were getting ready for bed. My mother gave a great laugh.

'Of course not, my dear. They're comrades, like ourselves,' she replied.

In reconsidering it years later I understood that our hosts belonged to the upper echelons of the East German *nomenklatura*. My father had met the husband during his doctoral studies in Moscow: some fingers of his right hand were missing, because he had shot them off himself when he had been conscripted so that he did not have to fight on Hitler's side. After prisoner-of-war camp he found himself at university where, among other things, he learned Hungarian. On the odd occasions he visited us in Budapest he would fool around with us children, in high spirits, but the one time we stayed with him and his wife in Berlin he seemed distracted and reserved and always had to be going off somewhere. Soon after the régime change of 1989 the couple both died, quite suddenly. They disappeared without ceremony: it was as if they wished to leave absolutely no trace, as if they had never existed, much like their country, the GDR.

The other lesson I learned on my first trip abroad was that the world was divided into two. On the outskirts of Berlin stood an enormous tower from whose top one could see another country. That other country was also called Germany. There was West and there was East, my parents explained. We learnt in school that the sun set on the left and rose on the right, but I didn't really understand why this made them two different countries, with the same name on top of them. Our parents took us to see the Wall, too. It was high, made of brick topped with barbed wire, and ran between two great look-out towers. Some six feet or more away there was another one. Between them a red circle.

'What's that red circle?' I asked uneasily.

'A soldier died there,' replied my mother.

'Why?'

'Because he was shot.'

'Who shot him?'

'Those who wanted to get over the wall.'

'Where?'

'To the other side.'

'Why? Aren't people allowed to?'

'What do you think the wall is for?'

'What is it for?'

'We have to defend ourselves.'

Since we happened to be in Berlin, our parents also took us to see the concentration camp at Sachsenhausen. In the taxi there they quickly explained what we were going to see. When the man with the funny moustache was in power that is where they took people they wanted to kill, those innocents who did not agree with him. There was no mention of the fact that a good part of our own family finished up in places like this. The man with the funny moustache was Hitler. Hitler's name was not to be mentioned the entire time we were in Germany so as not to offend our hosts. Why? Because they might think we held them to blame. But it wasn't them. The people who had done the dreadful things we had seen in Soviet movies lived on the other side of the Wall. The people this side were decent people. I saw the piles of human hair, the shaving brushes, the worn-down shoes. I saw the lampshades made of human skin. I saw the huts with their tiered bunks, the shower rooms whose walls were scrubbed white. On the way back in the taxi, in the amber-coloured afternoon light, I was shouting with all the fury a seven-year-old can muster.

'That swine! That rotten swine! The rotten swine!'

Now I understood why we needed that high brick wall with its barbed wire.

What was my father feeling when, with his usual rigour, he examined those bunks, the *Appelplatz* and the narrow paved path to the gas chambers? Did he say anything to my mother as they crept between the stiff cold sheets on Auntie Gerda's bed?

ᨖ

One afternoon on the metro, on my way to the hospital, I was reaching into my bag for something to read when my hand stopped in mid-air. It suddenly occurred to me that there might be someone among my bored fellow travellers whose face would turn into a dripping mask of hate if I happened to take the Jewish magazine, *Saturday*, from my bulging backpack. What hostility might I rouse in this pale green carriage – manufactured by Mytischinskiy Mashinostroitielny Zavod, as homely and warm as a pigsty, if I were to sit there holding hands with a black man. Or with a Roma boy, because in his case you couldn't even pretend he was some rich foreigner. In Geneva I simply cannot understand the sense of natural reserve that separates people from each other; in Hungary, though, I am always shocked by how quickly people lose their temper, the sheer fury that erupts when someone emits an innocent, but apparently wrong, signal. Whenever I come home, I feel a sense of blissful relaxation and the sudden outbursts of such fury hit me like a cold shower. So, by way of compromise, instead of *Saturday* I pulled out a copy of *HVG*, the Hungarian equivalent of *The Economist*. It's a small country choking on its own hatred, I told myself in a foul mood.

'So this is the democracy you wanted!' my father screamed, purple-faced, one Sunday lunch after the régime change.

Hegel, Gegel and Bebel grinned in satisfaction. They loved it when we lost our tempers. A terrible political brawl ensued. It was only hours after, once the combatants had tired of the shouting and, exhausted by my mother's feast, had declared a ceasefire, that my father was capable of telling us what had upset him so. Some days earlier he had been sitting on the 49 tram when a middle-aged man had clearly and loudly addressed him.

'You, yes, you, you stinking Jew! How come you weren't burned to a cinder at Auschwitz?'

'What?' we gasped and went pale. 'And what did other people say?'

'They carried on looking out of the window, just as they did in '44. A few kids were chortling away in the background.'

'And you? Did you say anything?'

'I got off the tram and walked home.'

The walk home from the Gellért Hotel to Németvölgyi Road can be very long. And then we had no idea that this was just the start. At that time it was still unacceptable to taunt Jews and gypsies: the new régime tried to wash its hands of any such unfortunate incidents. The language and style of newly awoken racism had not yet been elevated to the parlance of everyday politics as they were by the time of the third democratically elected government after 1998. Luckily my father did not survive to see that. But the beginnings were enough for him.

As far as my father was concerned Jewishness was a form of atavism. Not only because survivors of the war were of the generation that had tried to rip from their very being the ties that bound them to the terrible exterminations, but because he was convinced that if he redefined himself as a communist that would trump every other definition. Although after his death all the documents we found in his study showed that precisely the opposite was the case, he claimed that he had never worn a yellow star, was never deported and, apart from one unsuccessful attempt to enter the great synagogue at Dohány Street, had never been in the ghetto. He once indignantly told the story of how, in 1944, the illegal communists had smuggled him into the ghetto where he tried to persuade its occupants to undertake a Warsaw-type uprising. Being ejected from the foul-smelling, corpse-covered synagogue by his fellow Jews confirmed him in his opinion that he had done well to distance himself from them once and for all.

As I discovered later, this story was probably true but with one significant difference: my father had not been smuggled into the ghetto but had actually been living inside it when he tried to persuade the others to action. But his own version of events must have become fixed in his mind and was not to be shifted. According to his writings he survived by becoming an illegal communist and taking part in the underground resistance to fascism, using forged papers. What he didn't mention is that those papers were obtained for him by his mother from the Swedish Embassy. It wasn't just the religious aspect of Judaism my father rejected; he hated hearing Israel mentioned and always spoke of Jews in the third person. That is, bar one occasion in 1990 when someone in the new, freely elected parliament suggested that the speaker, a person of Jewish background, should be given a barrel to stand on. I had returned from England that morning and was about to move on to a conference in Prague in the evening. My mother and I were standing on the twilit platform of the Western Railway Terminal when my father turned up. I was touched that he wanted to see me. In the few minutes we had together we quickly gabbled out our respective most important news, at which point my father, for the first and last time in his life, said: 'They're after us again.'

It was a cool October evening and we could already see our breath before us. Maybe it was the sharp smell of smoke, or the rumbling of the train about to depart, or maybe it was because he was disorientated by the brevity of our meeting and the suddenness of our farewell, but it brought out the first person plural in my father. 'They're after us again' he said and in my shock I grabbed the cold handrail of the carriage door and buried my face in my scarf. I had waited decades for a sentence in which he dared claim the past as his own, to admit who he was and thereby let me know who I was: it reconnected us to our history, even if that history has been flooded with tears for centuries; it established us as part of a community, even if that community had been decimated time and again and even if we could only relate to a relatively small section of it. We were of that community and from this time forth the fact was established. Proceeding from that fact we could set out on whatever path our consciences dictated. We stood in the orange light of the evening lamps, wrapped in the autumn mist and the cloud of our own breath, silently glancing at each other. Then the conductor gave a loud whistle and I leapt up on to the slippery carriage step. The train slowly started to move off. I watched my father waving awkwardly from the platform, his figure shrinking to a speck in the cold neon light. I stood in the corridor for hours, shattered, staring out into the approaching night, watching the trees beyond the rails as they rushed backwards.

I know it is mere coincidence, of course, but the hyperactive myth-producer who shares the tenancy of my brain with its socialist realist counterpart can't help remarking that it was at the end of this particular journey that I met the man who ever since then has been sharing my life.

In what remained of his life my father had one last painful opportunity to shoulder the burden of his Jewishness. It was when, through no fault of his own, he read Imre Kertész's *Fatelessness*. This must have been near the beginning of the 1990s, when he paid us a visit in Geneva. One sleepy afternoon, at a most unexpected moment, the past suddenly grabbed my father by the throat and squeezed it with an iron fist, compelling him to confront facts he had succeeded in avoiding – facts that, owing to his good fortune, he had declared were, as far as he personally was concerned, non-facts. According to my father the fate of the Jews in the Second World War was a natural product of the murderous capitalist system, one of a long series of similarly awful, hidden or overt genocides that he, being a communist, utterly condemned as a matter of principle, but which had nothing to do with him. But that late spring day, in our apparently innocent home in Geneva, running his eyes over our chaotic bookshelves, my father stumbled across a minefield. Having woken from his afternoon nap while my mother and I were taking the children for a walk in the park, my father was looking for something to read when fate, in its usual arbitrary way, happened to guide him to *Fatelessness* in the old paperback edition, the one with the etching of Dürer's *Melancholia* on the cover. The book was a gift from my friend Tamás, who had presented it to me some years before as one of the undiscovered treasures of twentieth-century Hungarian literature, but I had not yet had the time to read it.

Chance had guided two very minor characters of that still incomprehensible and unforgivable drama that took place some fifty years before into the same darkening kitchen: my father, who now sat at the table crouched over the book with his head in his hands; he who had had the great good fortune to avoid what posterity was to call the Holocaust so it should not have to live with even more uncomfortable nominations; and the survivor whose story was presented in the book and who had not been able to escape the clutches of fate and who, decades later, decided to give an account of what it is like when the experience of hell fills every last pore of your being. My father certainly had read some pieces of 'Holocaust literature', among them the Spanish writer Jorge Semprún's *The Long Voyage*, written before Comrade Semprún strayed into the swamps of Eurocommunism – an act that rendered him *persona non grata* on our bookshelves, and the books of Mária Ember and Béla Zsolt that relate their experiences of deportation, but whenever he read such texts he carefully prepared himself in advance so that he would know into which secret recess of his consciousness to lock the terror so that it would not destroy him.

But that late afternoon in Geneva, in a foreign city, surrounded by foreign languages, when this book, written in Hungarian and with an attractive female figure shown deep in meditation on its front, fell into his hands, for a moment his guard went down. And by the time he realised the book was about him, about that bright-eyed, solitary adolescent boy with a desire to live, about those separated parents, about a father killed in the course of forced labour, about his own family before fate in the form of an Arrow Cross or a Nazi uniform struck them down, it was too late. He couldn't escape the power of nightmare. He was terminally caught in the looking-glass labyrinth, at every turn of which he was obliged to confront the image of himself which he had been trying all his life to avoid, whose very memory he wanted to wipe from the memory of the world, of which he was as terrified as he might have been of fire and brimstone. One glance of that condemned young boy who my father himself had been was enough to bring down the walls of ideology, lies and self-defence he had erected around himself for decades.

Wandering through that labyrinth initially he might have known precisely what was the difference between himself and his intangible mirror image. After a while, though, he couldn't have been at all certain who was the figure coming to meet him in the glass: he himself or his condemned likeness; he wouldn't have known which was him, or who he actually was; which of his movements was genuine and which an optical illusion; or whether there was anyone at all behind the cold surface of the mirror, someone playing a ruthless trick on him, a light-fingered being stripping him of his carefully protected life, repossessing it as though it were a coat he had borrowed then stolen; or whether all this was just illusion, a joke in bad taste. The game turned into a hunt, a pursuit from which there was no guarantee he could escape alive. It must have taken a considerable time for my father, running ever faster, gasping for air, and after various painful bumps into the walls of the labyrinth, finally to find the way out.

I discovered him in the dark kitchen, bent over the table, his face in his hands. When I called his name he raised his head and looked round him in confusion. His breath was coming a little fast and his eyes were wider than usual, as if he had just woken. He might have been crying but I couldn't tell because I had never seen him crying before and so did not know how his face would change when he was about to cry. I turned on the light and quickly started bustling about so as to bring him back to reality. He continued sitting motionless at the table gripping the closed book in his hand as if afraid that the dark demon might leap out of it again.

Some hours later, once we had put the children to bed, I asked him if he didn't feel like getting some fresh air. We went for a walk on the windy lake shore. Slowly, silently, we ambled under the lilac sky, waiting for the streetlights to be turned on.

'Well, I suppose we could call that a masterpiece,' my father suddenly spoke up.

Since this wasn't the kind of thing he tended to say, I

didn't want to push the matter by suggesting that if that was the case why didn't we call it just that. I started asking him about the book but his answers were brusque and he quickly changed the subject.

It was another seven years before I got round to reading *Fatelessness* myself. I had read Kertész's other books, treading warily through them so as to explore the territory and check out what was waiting for me. But whenever I took out *Fatelessness* and opened it at the part where the central character pushes the plate away at dinner and feels nauseous when his father touches him, I had to put the book down. And so it was several years before I understood what had happened to my father that afternoon in Geneva. Beyond the dramatic chance meeting of two survivors over a kitchen table, two visions of the world had also collided: the messianic dream of changing the world and the poetry of absolute zero. It was the belief in progress, the faith in humanity's march towards enlightenment against the reality stripped naked and robbed of its high calling. The freezing cold of absolute nothingness.

I had only the faintest acquaintance with the latter school of thinking. My father had looked to take my ideological orientation in hand early in my childhood, but my education in philosophy stopped at about the age of thirteen with Giordano Bruno. His example offered evidence of how retrograde forces deal with the representatives of progressive thought. Having got me to this point, my father considered I was ready to take a cavalier leap to what was properly essential, the reading of *The Critique of the Gotha Programme* and the *Communist Manifesto*, before proceeding on to other selected works of Marx, Engels and Lenin. None of these were as dramatically satisfying as the poor torched Italian for whom I wept hot tears at night, but – or so it seemed then – they offered a more direct path to human bliss.

My understanding of the history of ideas being relatively shallow, you may imagine how taken aback I was ten years later when, on a university summer camp studying *Das Kapital*, the major work of that epoch-making thinker Karl Marx, employing the critical tools worthy of a distinguished Yeshiva student, a guest professor of philosophy suddenly embarked on a reading of the Greek philosopher Parmenides. It was the first time I was confronted by the proposal, from a credible source, that life had no meaning. But, owing to my upbringing and natural inclination, I did not feel it necessary to pursue this line of thought more thoroughly. That is, until I read *Fatelessness*. Young Köves's story presents us with a life as stripped down to essentials as the axioms of Parmenides. Here was someone who had travelled down the whole road to the bourn from which no traveller returns, registering everything, and had rendered an account of his experiences twenty years after. But even after twenty years he was determined not to complain of any suffering, despair or even involvement. He catalogued the range of actions of which man was capable: what man might commit and what he might endure. By way of an afterword he added that once it was over his characters would not be ennobled, none would be judged or sanctified. Time would remain indifferent to them as it moved on and would sweep them all away, like litter.

My father's entire life had, on the other hand, been driven by the conviction that everything was imbued with meaning, that progress was irreversible and that mankind could be saved. The fact that he could conceive only of one kind of salvation and that he found it acceptable, indeed desirable, that people should be saved even despite themselves was a different matter. Dictatorship was justified because the masses weren't sufficiently mature to know what was good for them. We will beat you over the head with the club of salvation until your head hurts! But his blind faith in human goodness and progress at the heart of his political outlook was what made my father loveable. Even when I most strongly disagreed with both his views and his actions, I had to struggle so he did not entangle me in the web of our deepest common concerns and so make me his disciple.

If my father had been prepared for the low blow that *Fatelessness* dealt him he would have rejected it in the sacred name of progress and declared in his usual passionate way that its world view was simply existential nonsense. He would have put the book neatly back on our jumbled shelves and dismissed its author as another person whose thought, experience and ideas were irrelevant because they were false. But this time it was the voice of the child that spoke to him out of the misty past, his old self, or the best friend of his youth. And he simply could not kill that child in him. He had to hear the child through, in an audition that cost him many sleepless nights. Eventually, he got over this as well.

Author's Advice to Reader: Beware of gift books with attractive covers!

☙

My sister and I lived in blissful ignorance of our origins for some time. We were deeply familiar with the countless episodes of our mother's life but all we knew of our father's either consisted of some colourful tales of his father who had been martyred in the cause of socialism or were stories about our wicked grandmother. Our parents brought us up to be the products of enlightened communism and to believe that birth, skin colour and gender meant nothing because all were equal. So it never occurred to me that I was a Jew, nor would it have if there had not always been someone in every one of the important places in my life, from primary school through to places of work, to remind me and then go on to conclude that I must therefore be different. In what respect 'different' depended on where I happened to be and it was not necessarily unpleasant. There were moments when my finest academic achievements were attributed to my genes but also the time when a close childhood friend informed me that she would no longer be in touch because her new husband found the smell of my genes repulsive.

Practically no one talked about Jewishness in Hungary at that time. It wasn't mentioned in my family or among my circle of friends or in public discussions, so I was always astonished when someone brought it up. The world outside, as usual, seemed to be better informed on the subject than I was. At the beginning I would quietly walk home and ask my parents whether we were Jews.

'We are not Jews, because Judaism is a religion and we are atheists,' came the answer, and that put all my doubts to rest.

The murky issue of my origins was of no concern to me when, one fine August morning, I set out for Poland. I had spent the whole summer working in a brick factory in Óbuda, an old district of Budapest, saving up for my first independent trip abroad. I would be travelling for a month, hitchhiking, walking or on public transport, in that soulful, vibrant country full of life-changing energy. I must have been lucky, because it wasn't an altogether happy time there, but I found my every encounter enriching. Looking back on the early 1970s, they seem an age of innocence now.

One day my travels found me in Kraków. It had been raining for days and I was soaked through: the damp seemed to be inside me. I was hungry and tired and did not feel like talking to strangers or discovering great sights any more. I was fed up with the world and its wonders. I checked in at a youth hostel and threw myself on the bed to stare at the ceiling for days. I heard the rain drumming on the window and felt life slowly leaking away from me. Everything that had seemed important was being washed away with the rivers of water flowing down the open drain outside. The mere thought that I had anything to do with this chaotic mess of a world seemed quite absurd.

On the fourth day I dragged myself down to the diner on a nearby street, ordered a steaming coffee and forced myself to think of setting off again. I slouched through the wet streets without enthusiasm. But then, as I turned from the river embankment into a warren of narrow streets, a light suddenly flashed above the roofs shrouded in grey. Tentatively at first, then with ever greater conviction, the sun started shining. It was as if I had just woken up: I began to notice the beauty of the town. There was the perfectly preserved medieval square with its smooth cobbles and figures of saints carved out of stone, surrounded by colourful roofs with mosaic tiles. Close by there were women in headscarves and apprentices in leather caps bustling through the busy market. I bought a few greengages from an old stallholder and walked on, quite cheered up. It was only as I was leaving the square that I noticed I had walked on to what seemed like a film set. In a corner of the square, at the turning of a narrow passage, hung a worn old tin sign saying: *Synagogue*. Under it was an arrow pointing to the right. Might as well see this, too, I said to myself, and looked round for somewhere to dispose of the greengage stones. The synagogue was a freshly painted white building at the side of a small nearby square. I knocked at the iron gate, then cautiously rang the bell. After a little while a beautiful young woman in a long skirt opened the gate. Behind her stood a slightly shorter girl with very fair hair who looked a bit like her, as if they were sisters.

'Good day,' I said. 'I'd like to look inside.'

'I'm afraid we're not open yet,' the girl replied courteously. She was going to close the gate but, since I hadn't moved, she added: 'The opening is at the beginning of next week.'

I thought to tell her that I wouldn't be here in a week's time, but in the end it didn't seem too important. I stood indecisively in the doorway. I could easily have left but my foot seemed fixed somehow. The girl looked at me in expectation. I felt a confused apologetic smile form on my lips. I cleared my throat but still I could not decide whether to push my luck further now that I was here or just turn round, as befits a well-mannered stranger, and let her close the gate. The girl was watching me carefully. Then suddenly she said: 'Well, if you really want to, come in.'

There was a touching courtesy in the way the Polish people addressed me in the third person and called me 'young lady'. I didn't speak Polish, but my by-then substantial knowledge of Russian and my general desire to understand everything made communication possible. I stepped into the empty hall, ringing with silence and thick with the smell of paint, and politely walked around it. In the middle stood a podium surrounded by some wrought- iron rails: it must be the place where they read the Bible, I thought.

'There is an exhibition in the other room, if you're interested,' said the girl.

I went into the room next door. Against the sparkling white wall were placed glass cabinets containing photographs and a few objects associated with what had been Jewish life in Kraków. I examined everything thoroughly. There was only the sound of my footsteps in the hall and the rapid whispering of the two girls in the background. The last cabinet contained some photographs of the deportations. The streets I had walked down looking for a litter basket were being trodden by a mass of people with suitcases and packs. I examined each face separately. My eyes fell, from time to time, on a photograph showing a middle-aged woman walking down the middle of the road by herself. It was impossible to tell whether she was part of any of the groups marching beside her. She was holding her coat together with one hand and clutching a suitcase with the other. Her headscarf had slipped back over her hair, and she was gazing ahead with a serious look of calm on her face. This woman with her tumbling hair might be your grandmother, a voice said inside me. Or you. My gaze was fixed on the photograph of the unknown woman as if I thought that with a single glance I could pluck her out of the destruction waiting for her at the end of the journey. The next moment I was standing over the cabinet with my hands over my face, rocking to and fro, like someone about to fall. My whole body was shaken by a silent sobbing. After a while the chattering stopped behind me. As soon as I noticed it I put my backpack down, pulled out a handkerchief and loudly blew my nose. Then I carefully zipped the bag up, smiled at the two girls and turned to leave. When they opened the gate I looked round at them once more and succeeded in grunting:

'Thank you.'

'We thank you,' said the one with the darker hair. Her hand was resting on the gate handle as if she were waiting for something.

I stepped out into the square that was flooded with sunlight now. I stood for a while by the white walls, then, as if afraid that something might yank me back, I set off again with uncertain steps.

I think it was that afternoon I decided I was a Jew. The constant unnamed absence inside me touched the solid sense of gaping loss that haunted those abandoned streets of old Kraków and I understood where I belonged and what it was that had eluded me.

On my return home I felt a deeply Freudian missionary zeal to do everything in my power to lead my father back to his broken Jewish roots. I read the relevant critical literature, visited all the appropriate historical sites, brought him Purim cakes from the Fröhlich pâtisseries, hoping to ignite his Proustian reflexes. Unfortunately my father's reflexes tended more towards the Pavlovian: he ate the cakes but they made him no keener to delve into the past. Finally, having exhausted all my ideas and growing increasingly embittered, I asked him bluntly why not. His answer was that, as far as he was concerned, the Jewish question had lost its historical relevance and was no more than a display of tribal affiliation that, fortunately, had nothing to do with him since, owing to the early development of his consciousness, he regarded himself as a member of a universal movement whose goal was the liberation of the world, not as a member of some particular section of society. Pretty much like Marx, he added with due modesty.

I had no answer to this argument and was obliged simply to shut up and stop questioning my father's sense of superseded identity, particularly since I also regarded myself as being a member of the same universal movement for world liberation. Yet I could not forget that more specific identity. After a long internal struggle I finally concluded that, unlike in the archaic past, Jewishness today was a matter of commitment, not blood. Identities determined by blood relations are always dubious anyway and often result in terrible atrocities.

For a while I continued to bombard my father with cakes, but no longer to any ulterior purpose, simply because, like every other survivor I knew, he had a very sweet tooth. But eventually there was no need for that either. The first time he fell ill my mother turned her back on her vice-rectorial chair at the university where she taught in order to focus all her energies on caring for him. One aspect of this was that she perfected her knowledge of cake-baking technology and soon surpassed even the Fröhlich pâtisseries.

All this would have looked different had the world in which we actually lived given a fig for my father's theoretically justified sense of political consciousness and did not constantly rub his nose into the fact of his Jewishness. Clad in the armour of his superior ideological convictions, my father generally ignored this. And yet I am not altogether certain that he did not suffer it at a visceral level to the end of his life. That is to say, partly on account of the insults and partly because he had no home to go to.

The second disturbing gift I brought back from my Polish trip and put down in front of my father was of a political nature. All those countless people who helped me along the way, gave me accommodation, carefully showed me round, explaining everything, from a bus driver through to a university lecturer, were – every one of them – opposed to the system, as we put it then. They asserted, perfectly calmly and in a clear and objective manner, that it wasn't the first time in history that a lying oppressive political power had taken control of their lives, a power against which they were obliged to protest by means of art, political association and refusal to serve in the army; by cultivating small garden plots; by attending jazz concerts; through sexual liberation; by any means whatsoever. This clear-sighted, calm but firm conviction had an enormous effect on my dawning consciousness. That is to say, naturally, until I got home and talked to my father, who immediately set about putting me right again. But this first memory of political rebellion, as well as, to me, the quite unaccustomed sense of dignity such people radiated because they had taken responsibility for their own lives and made their decisions on the basis of free conscience, made a lifelong impression on me.

My first Polish trip also revealed that we Hungarians were not the biggest losers in creation. When we were children, on top of all the mangled texts we had to learn as part of our proletarian internationalist tasks, we sang our passionate way through the '*Himnusz*', our national anthem, the '*Szózat*' – Mihály Vörösmarty's 'Appeal' to his fellow Hungarians – and the burning verses of our national poet Sándor Petőfi which we of course interpreted in the then-common, purely literal sense. In this way, without realising it, we grew up with the enforced image of Hungary as a nation of incomparable talent that had undergone incomparable suffering and thus deserved the very best that fate could offer by way of recompense. In learning the various chapters of Poland's unhappy history I realised that it was possible to suffer even more intensely than we had done. (Much later I observed that all the nations of our region had a tendency to regard themselves as heroes or, alternatively, victims, depending on whatever needed justifying at the time.) Having mourned the bitter history of the Poles I recognised that suffering wasn't a matter of totting up numbers, and that it was pointless to compare losses and pains; they are immeasurable. What's more, suffering did not entitle you to anything. This last observation was to prove very useful in the future.

Decades afterwards, it dawned on me that the brick factory where I earned the money to pay for my tour of Poland, doing hard physical work in the happy days of my youth when unemployment existed only inside the factory and not outside, and undermined morale but not, as now, existence itself; in those days when physical work and the objects produced by intelligence, strength, skill and sweat still meant something and were a matter of honour; it was possible that this brick factory, of which remains now only its huge chimney, towering above the shopping parade of Bécsi Road offering the most glittering trophies of consumer society, was the same factory in which my fellow Jews from the outer suburbs were kept under guard all those years ago, before being piled on to the wagons. If that was the case, then this was also the very factory from which my great-aunt Gigi, who had given me the keys to the past one summer, had escaped, thereby avoiding Auschwitz – the same factory where I, quite unbothered by shades of the past, worked some twenty years later with blistered hands, trying to learn the ABC of the life of the proletariat. Now let someone tell me that things don't fit together.

☙

Maybe I should consider the possibility that the summer my father died began in the December of 1970, when Poland's then leader, Władysław Gomułka, ordered live bullets to be fired at workers protesting before the Gdańsk shipyard. Nineteen fifty-six might have been too soon after the war, when memory of deportations, starvation, freezing winters were still too fresh; the new power might still have appeared promising, without showing yet the cracks in the system. By 1968 you could perhaps have argued that the noble scheme of reforming socialism had taken an unfortunate turn. But after December 1970 you could not in all conscience insist that the people being shot at were just over-excited members of the intelligentsia, deluded students or rootless cosmopolitans. It was the ruling working class that took its stand in the shipyard at Gdańsk to demonstrate its discontent. And it is true that it was ruthlessly silenced then, but ten years later when the ruling working class once more downed tools to stand in the yard, the memory of those blazing guns rose like a bloody ghost and swept right across Eastern Europe. After December 1970 it was no longer possible to maintain the fiction that the workers were in power, that our high ideals were being realised. The reality was that it was in the name of those same high ideals that those whose condition was supposed to be the chief concern of the ideals were being shot.

It was in the early summer of 1981, when the latest struggle between society and authority was assuming ever more dramatic proportions, that my father went to Poland on a study trip. He arrived home early one morning. It must have been the exam season because I was dozing over sheaves of paper on my desk when he walked in.

'Hey, you're back already,' I remarked enthusiastically. 'How was Poland?'

Though we agreed on ever fewer matters by then, I always enjoyed hearing his accounts of his journeys, so full of minute observations. But that morning my father sat down on the chair next to me without a word and stared straight ahead with an empty look. He wagged his head from time to time, as if arguing with an invisible companion. When he finally looked at me his expression was as desolate as a house set for demolition.

'They've ruined everything,' he whispered, almost to himself.

I stared at him in shock. I had never seen him like this. Perhaps it was getting up so early or the fear of flying that rendered him so vulnerable. Or maybe something else had collapsed inside him.

'They shot the workers,' I whispered back. 'Imagine the dictatorship of the proletariat shooting down its own workers!'

At the time, the 1970 shootings at Gdańsk, like the Prague Spring, seemed to be a distant, incomprehensible event that had nothing to do with my life. And so it remained, until history brought them to mind again: my conscience needed time to catch up. In the feverish months of 1980 and 1981, while the whole Eastern Bloc was anxiously watching developments in Poland, the astonished Budapest intelligentsia was being flooded with handmade stencils filled with accounts of the 1970 shootings, the 1980 clandestine commemoration of the shootings, the documents of the KOR (the Workers' Defence Committee) and the fiery debates of Solidarność. The 1980 events in Gdańsk proved to me without doubt that the high-minded system in which I had firmly believed from childhood was, like Cronus, devouring its own children. But that morning, sitting opposite my father in the draughty children's room, I was not up to a decent political row, the kind that always ended in him steamrollering me. I tried to relax the tension by making a joke, but my whole body was shaken by an icy shivering. I think I feared that if doubt settled in his soul, if the great, apparently impregnable defences he had so carefully built around himself began to crack, there would be nothing to hold him together. But by the evening, once he had bathed, shaved and eaten and returned from the university, he had an explanation ready. And when, a couple of months later, General Jaruzelski with his dark glasses brought in a state of emergency in Poland, that was 'restoring order'.

Maybe it was that summer that his ideals and his sense of reality finally began to separate. It must have been a superhuman effort for him to persuade himself – and others – that, despite the firing squads, the arrests, the imprisonments and the conversion of a whole country into a sinister barracks, everything was all right, and that whatever was happening was simply a strict but justified course of action against dangerous and treacherous elements. It may be that the sources that sustain in a man, at least a man of my father's stamp, a belief in truth and sense of mission began to dry up in him. And in order to balance this clearly perceptible inner exhaustion, he had to use an ever more significant proportion of his energy to maintain appearances, which unavoidably swept him even further from reality and the world he still wanted to save. A decade later, when everything – even the last hollow appearances of the Cause – had collapsed, burying any distant prospect of a life not spent in the pursuit of money or suffering from the lack of it, forgetting every dream of dignity, freedom and community, my father continued to run through the ever-deepening quicksand of ideologised reality like a demented, blinkered, ear-stopped lunatic.

In the period of grace between my father's two bouts of illness, at the beginning of the 1990s, I found myself in Poland again. The geographic coordinates were familiar to me but the country itself was not. This was post-shock-therapy Poland, the economic success story, the laurelled victor of post-communist transition, the land of the so-called boundless possibilities promised by the market – and a profoundly depressing place. It was missing the assured dignity that had made such a deep impression on me in my adolescence. The freedom of inner resistance was replaced by the freedom to consume and an ever-less-meaningful choice between political hucksters; the overt, stupid suppression of the past having given way to a system of subtler, less transparent but almost limitless manipulation. And behind all this lay an infinite sadness. Just like at home.

I was in Kraków again, in the entirely restored Jewish quarter: the absences that had once broken my heart were filled out by stalls, Jewish bookshops, pâtisseries, fancy restaurants and gift shops: not even the Jews were missing, having arrived from every corner of the world, obediently trailing behind tour guides who were loudly explaining what the group should be looking at and what they should be moved by. I was hanging around in front of the synagogue again, with a tiny child in my womb preparing to be born, having either missed the Saturday morning service or been too embarrassed to go in, I no longer remember. On the basis of my visual memory I decided that this was definitely the same synagogue, but everything was different outside.

I went to a café and sat down, confused. Instead of rejoicing in the crisply renovated houses, I felt something was lost under the fresh plaster, that the little that remained of the past would from now be cheap pickings, that memory would serve a function that was new to me, one that had nothing to do with either the dead or the survivors. Suddenly, just as it had all those years ago, the sun came out. A young man holding the hand of a child was walking up one of the side streets that feed into the main square. The little boy was happily bouncing up and down beside his father. I recalled my own father's warm, enormous, bear-like paws into which I was delighted to slip my tiny hand in childhood and relaxed a little, taking a sip of my tea. When I looked up again, though, the street was deserted as if no one had walked that way for hours. I leapt to my feet as if I were hunted, quickly found a phone booth and rang my father.

'What's up?' he asked, his voice flat as if he had just got out of bed.

I could imagine him in the hall of the flat in Németvölgyi Road, sitting by the bookshelves and crouching over the phone in order to hear me better, doodling as we talked on the back of a beer mat he had brought home from one or other trip to Prague. I started to tell him where I was but then realised as I was speaking that the story was too long, too complicated.

'Nothing special,' I said eventually. 'Just ringing to see if everything is all right.'

We said goodbye and I put the phone down.

The day before leaving Poland, I walked round Warsaw a little. Here everything was new and blank. The Palace of Culture and Science rose above the dense traffic like a solitary scarecrow. Slightly sleepy and a touch distracted, like a well-meaning tourist, I noted the fruits of progress until I stumbled over the first black granite blocks marking the boundaries of the old ghetto. Immediately I woke up. I thought there was nothing left. I thought the whole ghetto had been razed to the ground, as in Robert Capa's famous photographs, and that the very name of Krochmalna Street had vanished. But it hadn't been razed to the ground and the name of the street was still there. And the two old buildings at the end with their rusty wrought-iron balconies hanging loose might have been left over from the time when Krochmalna Street was the centre of the universe for the young Isaac Bashevis Singer, and where some decades ago the leaders of the Warsaw uprising might have met.

I walked the street over and over, ever more slowly, as if looking for something. Stucco had been dropping off the tenement walls since time immemorial, there was graffiti by the gutted postboxes and the rotting salad and tins of Bulgarian baked beans in the greengrocer's window looked abandoned. The road widened surprisingly in the middle and I imagined the size of the crater remaining here when they blew up those elegant blocks. A little further up there was a 'garage': a vacant lot surrounded by fences guarding Western cars from the increasing number of people with sticky fingers; a wooden hut with a watchman inside listening to a crackling transistor radio, its batteries held in by elastic bands borrowed from jam jars. At the end of the street were some concrete tower blocks built in the 1960s, with their shattered decorative tiles and broken Venetian blinds on their cell-like bedrooms, where even dreams smelled liked boiled cabbage. Janusz Korczak's famous orphanage was somewhere around here, too, I suddenly remembered. Władysław Szpilman's memoirs, on which Roman Polanski's film *The Pianist* is based, tell of that bright August morning when the children set out with their nurses towards Umschlagplatz. What had Dr Korczak told his beloved charges so they could proceed so calmly towards the train that carried them to certain death? They were singing, as if out on an excursion. How could he have got them to suppress their fear and tension so they thought only of whose hand they should be holding, trying to remember the words of the song?

Adults can say whatever they like to children. For a long time in childhood an adult's words constitute the firmest reality. The words they hear can help children survive the most terrible ordeal, but can also cast them into the deepest despair. The same is true of what adults conceal. No one said anything to my father. Children were rarely regarded by that generation of parents as people one talked to. 'You'll understand when you grow up,' his father told him when they met for the last time at the café next to the Astoria in Budapest. 'I'll be back for you soon,' his mother told him by the fence of the foundling home in Szeged. My father received no parental advice on how to handle the universal catastrophe that would tear his entire life up by the roots. There was no survival handbook. Nor was there any available information about the new world being built on the smoking ruins of the old one, only what he read in Party pamphlets and in books of simplified Marxist-Leninism. He had to construct his own reality.

☙

My dear sister,

I was heartbroken not to see you, but at least you were away and I was here to stand watch over him, so we could change roles. I found Father in a reasonable state though there were a few alarming incidents. One day we were delivering something to a female comrade near Őrs Vezér Tere metro station. Having got off the train, it took half an hour to struggle up the stairs. On reaching the top Fülöp declared that we were in the wrong place and, before I could say anything, he had set off across the six-lane street. I tried desperately to yank him back but he was quite determined and pressed ahead among screeching brakes and drivers cursing us with a few choice words. When we reached the far side, our legs shaking, I asked him why he did that, but he just blinked at me as though he had no idea what I was talking about. When I repeated the question he said he couldn't bear to go down those stairs and up again.

By the way, we never did find the house. We spent at least an hour scouring the area: it must be here, just round that corner, where that tree is, or rather no, next to the tobacconist's. He hadn't brought the address with him, of course, because he thought he knew the way. The public phone boxes were either occupied or vandalised. By the time we found one the line was engaged, our mother having an endless conversation with someone. But she wouldn't have been able to open Father's locked drawers to find the address anyway. We turned round towards the raggedy market because Fülöp remembered that the female comrade helped out here in the afternoon, earning a little extra income to supplement her pension. We asked the stallholders but they stubbornly denied all knowledge of her. I was dead on my feet by then but he wouldn't give up. On the way to the underpass a nice gypsy guy from Salgótarján sold us a four-piece set of enamel saucepans that, Fülöp was immediately convinced, was the set of Mother's dreams. (I cannot begin to describe to you the face she pulled when we arrived with our booty.) While we discussed the incomparable workmanship of the enamel works at Bonyhád, Father busily gathered information about political and economic conditions in Salgótarján, the life story of the vendor, the condition of his housing and the fate of his children. The only reason he didn't get round to having the man sign his Party enrolment statement was that we were getting very cold. On the way home in the metro we leaned against each other panting under the weight of the saucepans. 'Well,' Fülöp remarked, 'at least we haven't completely wasted our time.' 'Oh absolutely not,' I answered, exhausted.

Our other adventures were not quite as colourful as this. The fact is, all the tests have proved negative. We're coming back at the end of June. Hold out till then!

Love,
Y

P.S. Yesterday we went to a concert at the very barracks-like conservatoire in Geneva. Márta and György Kurtág played

Bach, Bartók and some of their own compositions in between. I was quite blown away by that heavenly flow of music when suddenly the motif of 'The Ballad of Borbála Angoli' emerged: 'her lovely slender waist had thickened'. I simply burst into tears.

☙

My dear Miki,
If Odysseus is the archetype of the European soul we're all doomed. Odysseus learns nothing. After twenty years of adversity and suffering he returns to Ithaca not a whit different from how he left it, just as ruthless, vain and greedy as before. The first thing he does is to massacre everyone and would have immediately set about more bloodshed if Pallas Athene hadn't intervened. No doubt Odysseus is wily, curious and tenacious, but he is driven by nothing more than ambition and a desire to win. He never understands anything. Even his visit to his mama in the underworld is futile: her warnings go in one ear and out the other. That's not even to mention his skewed values and relationships. How can someone who has tricked and betrayed everyone he has ever met demand loyalty?

I far prefer Gilgamesh. In the beginning he is as ruthless and vain as Odysseus, but on his journey he encounters friendship, love and death and so he changes. By the time the story has ended it is a man's eyes we are looking into, someone whose gaze, even at a distance of three thousand years, sends cold shivers up our spines. Or my spine at least.

Hugs,
Y

Third

On the way to the hospital, while sitting on the metro and searching in my bag for a bottle of water or something to read, I came across my camera. 'How did this get here?' I wondered, though my backpack was so full I wouldn't have been surprised if I'd happened to fish a kangaroo out of it.

'What about taking some pictures of each other?' I asked my father one afternoon, trying to sound relaxed.

He immediately agreed. We took our places on the bed, him first then me, and we snapped each other. Despite the great heat in the room, I shivered. *Click-clack, click-clack.* My father in striped pyjamas, looking very thin, his head shaved, suddenly stared into the lens, absolutely clear-eyed. He is a convict on the run. *Click-clack, click-clack.* I am in a summer dress that has slipped to one side, my hair is a mess and I am gazing ahead with a confused expression. My eyes look questioning. The answer was in his eyes, but neither of us wanted to see it.

ᘓ

One bright May day, sometime near the end of the 1970s, two of Szera's surviving relatives – my great-aunt Gigi and great-uncle Harry – arrived without notice at the newly opened Forum Hotel in Budapest. Harry's twin, Larry, had only just died and his death probably played no small part in the others' decision to search out their mother's grave in Hungary. The twins were inseparable, it was said. They looked almost exactly like each other except that Harry (or Larry) was right-handed while the other, Larry (or Harry), was left-handed. They were lively boys of a bohemian bent, both exceptionally talented at table tennis. They even played competitively for a while, performing in exhibition matches in Europe: spectators found the sight of two handsome boys knocking the ball to and fro irresistibly attractive. In the spring of 1938 they were happy to respond to an invitation to play from over the ocean when they discovered that a blustering bully of an apprentice house painter called Schicklgruber had marched into the gracious city of Vienna where they had spent their carefree youth, and wanted to install a new régime there. The twins decided they would not return home for a while and, after a couple of years of being blown here and there, they settled in Australia, where, owing to the boundless opportunities offered by the New World, their own sound business sense and the ban on alcohol in the USA that made their strong, self-produced, Hungarian-style spirits highly popular in the ships that passed by, they quickly made it rich. It was not until the early 1970s that they returned to Hungary. They looked up my father but the meeting turned out to be somewhat on the cool side. Of course, since my two uncles were the very embodiment of capitalism, they couldn't understand my father's feelings: he paid them a courtesy visit at the luxurious Gellért Hotel and gave them a lot of useful tourist information, after which, as far as he was concerned, duty was done.

This time, however, Harry was accompanied by his wife, a refugee from Austria, and Gigi – that is, Aunt Giselle, my grandmother's favourite sister and my father's first love from when he was a little boy. Gigi must have been in her late seventies, but she was still a strikingly beautiful woman. It probably never occurred to her enchanted admirers, observing her drift astonishedly past the newly renovated palaces of the inner city, marvel at the children parading past her on their Sunday walk, or laugh with the waiters while ordering her cold cherry soup, from what depths this high-spirited and witty lady had emerged to return. She was like a mirror to the beauty around her.

Gigi was three when her mother died giving birth to the twins. She must have been a bright, lively little girl; perhaps she retained to the last some faint memory of the busy comings and goings of a house suddenly stricken by an incomprehensible catastrophe. But she clearly remembered the heavy silence that descended on the hall, and the sense of loss brought about by the absence of the soft, gentle body of her mother. Despite the urging of his friends and relatives, my great-grandfather had no wish to marry again and brought up nine children alone, with no more help than a solitary housekeeper. Once Gigi was a little older she would often tiptoe into his study, put her slender arms about his neck and read a little of the book open on his desk. Next to the book there was the picture of a woman of about forty gazing back at the photographer with a sad, polite little smile. Gigi had long forgotten those soft almond-coloured eyes and the dark, heavily tumbling hair; she knew only the stories told about her mother, and the tight feeling she faintly felt in her stomach, though she couldn't precisely tell whether the sadness was caused by the unknown woman, her father, or something else. She pressed her face into her father's tobacco-smelling beard and worked her arms around his neck as if afraid that a storm might be brewing over the fields, one that might wipe out everything around her. Then the pair of them stood up, slightly embarrassed, and went about their business, the man to oversee the workers in the fields and the girl to tend to her younger brothers.

The storm arrived some thirty years later, taking almost everything with it: the estate, the house, the books, the photographs, and the family. The only thing Gigi was left with was the tight sense in her stomach that there were still people to bury. She was over seventy when suddenly, out of the mists of time, emerged a man who had been through similarly shattering experiences, and whom she might have loved anew. But his heart literally stopped at such a prospect of happiness. Gigi accepted the role of mourner with a veteran's resilience.

'Do you think it strange that a person can fall in love at seventy or more? That she can cry like an adolescent? After everything that has happened?' she asked me thoughtfully in her hospital bed.

From the lofty heights of near thirty I did not find it at all strange. There was nothing in anything she said that struck me as strange. But this conversation was to take place much later. At our first meeting in Budapest, when I was in my early twenties, I followed Gigi about everywhere, as if under a spell. I clung to her every word, her every breath: I was like a plant seeking rain. And I saw my father too was under some spell when he was near her. His usual reserve in society melted away. Instead of a comradely handshake, he embraced her and the other members of the exiled family, laid aside political differences, showered them with countless clumsy tokens of attentiveness, from signed copies of his works exploring the deep structure of really-existing socialism to bottles of the finest Hungarian spirits; in other words, he did everything he could to be a warm and generous host. But I saw how, at the same time, he was doing his best to elbow aside the past, trying not to recognise in this delicate and scented old lady the beautiful woman of his youth whom he had once chosen, instead of his mother, as the woman of his dreams. There was just the one occasion, I think, when by chance he was left alone with Gigi in the hotel lobby. They were quietly sitting next to each other on the soft velvet settle, my father probably feverishly searching for some harmless topic of conversation, when her graceful wrinkled hands stroked his face and her eyes searched whatever lay behind the awkwardly smiling eyes and those dry but still splendidly curved lips whispered meditatively:

'Phil, dear little Phil.'

No one ever addressed my father like this. We didn't immediately know who she was talking about. It was still more incomprehensible that he answered. We didn't know he was called by this name in childhood; we doubted he ever had a childhood. As far as we were aware, his story started when his wicked mother left him at that home in Szeged and continued with his admission into the steely ranks of the workers' movement. And no one there ever called him 'little Phil'.

When the family delegation led by Gigi first appeared, I am sure my father was frozen with terror rather than full of the euphoria of reunion. He had the survivor's infallible instinct for danger and immediately took the necessary steps to forestall it. It is true that he behaved impeccably whenever he was around them, but he would always claim that he had too much work on and hide behind the insurmountable walls of his study. When it came to meals, he would either arrive late or leave early and, if I remember right, he even managed to organise an official visit to the provinces while they were there. He hid away whenever he was able, as if he had an unpleasant skin disease he didn't want the others to see. That disease was the past that, despite iron curtains, despite all his precautions and attempts at obscurity, managed to break in on him from across the ocean and politely knock at his door in the figure of an entrancing old woman. And since my father was always officially away, I took time off from my university studies to spend a couple of days with my unknown relatives. I walked along the Danube embankment with Gigi, though when I noticed that she was shivering I put my arms around her and gently guided her to a side street, away from the river whose waters had flown red the last time she had seen it, so many Jews had been shot and pushed into it by the gangs of the Arrow Cross. I stumbled across the still untidy yard of the great Dohány Street synagogue with them; I pressed into Gigi's hands copies of Miklós Radnóti's prose memoir *Under Gemini*, which talks about his mother and his twin brother (who died at birth), and his *Bori Notebook*, the volume of his great last poems found after he was killed on a death march.

My mother and I took our distinguished visitors out to their village of origin where my great-grandfather – the enlightened Zionist and democrat, faithful Jew and proud Hungarian patriot – once, so I was astonished to discover, owned an estate. We wandered, the three old folk, my mother and I, among the neglected Jewish cemetery's leaning, moss-covered stones to find the object of their journey, the grave of my great-grandmother who had died giving birth to the twins.

'Kup-fer-stein Ce-cí-li-a.' Gigi spelled out the Hebrew name in a trance, her long, ringed fingers stroking the stone as if it were alive.

My poor father never suspected that, just as he was carefully moving into the fringe world of underground resistance, a timed explosive device was being planted in his warm and secure home. Gigi quickly discovered that she had found a keen and faithful listener in me. Since her own young son, along with all children of similar age, had been sent to the ovens in Auschwitz, and since the members of the family born in Australia after the war neither understood Hungarian nor showed any great interest in the confused and bloody past of their parents who had fled from Europe, Gigi felt that she had to tell the family story to someone before it completely vanished into the mists of time. It was not that I was the person most fit to hear it, it was simply that I was the nearest to hand. My sister was abroad legally, with a passport and official permission. There were no other descendants. I, for my part, was enormously grateful to receive this precious heritage. After almost twenty-five years of groping around in the dark, suddenly I had something tangible to hold on to: there was a grave with Hebrew letters, there were names, dates and stories that were part of my own past, of what I myself was. I pushed the scrappy yellow school notebook in which every night I scribbled down everything Gigi told me in front of my father.

'This is what Gigi said. Is it true?'

It was true. True, true, and true. It was all true. Without meaning to, Gigi had knocked a hole in the carefully constructed and a hundred-times reinforced fortress that my father had built to protect himself from a great deal of pain and uncomfortable truth. At the same time, she was putting yet another nail in my father's coffin. Not that the facts would have changed his attitude towards reality. When he died, twenty years later, he still could not bring himself to say that his mother had not rejected him but had tried to save him, and that it was not because of his socialist beliefs but because he was Jewish that his father had been transported to the labour camp. That the battle he had fought all his life, neglecting everything and everyone for it, was not the battle for which he had first staked his life, but the direct opposite.

A couple of years after our first dramatic and euphoric encounter, Gigi invited me to Australia to meet the other survivors and those born after the war. I found her in a hospital bed on her last legs. Her liver-spotted, ever elegant hands gently slid into mine and she shook her head in incredulity when one afternoon I arrived with a portable tape recorder. I pulled a cassette of Katalin Karády songs from my pocket and popped it into the machine. In Hungary we had entered an era of gradual liberalisation that no one suspected would lead to the collapse of the régime. Karády, a diva who had been at the height of her fame between the two wars, was no longer a disgraced collaborator, someone banished from national memory, but a souvenir of the tolerated past, to become fifteen years later a hero of national resistance. Before my Australian trip I recorded on cassette an album of her greatest hits that had just been released and threw it into my suitcase when I was packing.

'Do you remember this? Do you know it?' I asked Gigi while listening to that low, velvety voice in the private room fully supplied with all the comforts, a room, as I was later to discover, quite close to the one in which my unknown grandmother had died so many years before. Gigi gave a loud laugh. She had a week left of life. Her head turned to one side, her eyes half-closed, with a dreamy smile she sang along with the cassette: 'Where is that summer, where is that old love of mine?'

A few days later she fell into a coma. She stopped reacting to the outside world, and started to communicate only with her inner one. I sat in a chair in the corner of the room, silently observing the peculiar dance of unknown friends and relatives as they made their way on tiptoe to the bed and out again, nodding to them as they left. I sat hugging the wall and listening to the cascade of words as her life unrolled like a film. I heard her exchanging words with her dead mother; with her father who sometimes, when he thought no one was looking, stood at the window of the dining room and wept for his late wife; her young son, who was dispatched to his grandmother in the country in order to ensure his safety, but who was then packed in a wagon and sent to Poland; her siblings, some of whom vanished into the gas chambers while others fell prey to sickness; her beloved first husband, who avoided deportation by joining the resistance in the hills of Slovakia, only to have to escape the pogrom after the war in the small highland town to which he returned to search for his deported family, but who then died in Australia, on the operating table, as a result of a surgical error before he could begin a new life in a new country; the second husband who, having survived everything, one day simply gave up on life. Even my never-encountered grandparents appeared in the film of her life; she seemed to have failed to convince my famously obstinate grandfather of something. I listened with bated breath. I trembled in case the stream of words should come to a stop and we should suddenly find ourselves suspended in the cold air, 'perched on the branch of nothing'. I knew I was lucky to hear it all, but I was also inconsolably sad because I knew she would die and that I would never see her again, and that the past would finally vanish with her, a past to which she was the last credible witness; because there was no way for me to see through her words; her ever more broken speech would not lead me towards those whom I could never meet; I could not even catch a glimpse of their faces: they were all about to disappear for ever.

'What is she saying?' the sympathetic young doctor in charge of my great-aunt asked when he dropped in.

'She is remembering,' I whispered.

'In what language?' the doctor asked.

'Hungarian,' I replied, but my throat was too dry to say more.

It was as if the language, whose infinite beauty we only discovered when we were thousands of miles from the country where everyone on the street speaks it naturally, had become a last refuge where Gigi could hide one last time, a refuge in which I crouched next to her, along with her best friend Éva, who was herself at the edge of madness. Having only recently attended her own husband's funeral, Éva still visited Gigi every day and we hugged and consoled each other in our secret language before she left to avoid being crushed completely by this second inevitable blow.

One day Éva took me for lunch in an elegant waterside restaurant. We took our places at the immaculate damask-covered table and Éva ordered some fish speciality. We sat in the calm sunshine of what, to me, was an unfamiliar city in an unknown corner of the world, the waiters gliding elegantly this way and that as if on skates. The chinking of glasses and the purr of the coffee machine blended gently with the murmur of the regular guests. Éva was telling me, in choice Transylvanian terms, what it was like to be on the death march from Auschwitz to Breslau. The exquisite fish dish tasted like a single, under-differentiated salty mass. I put on my dark glasses, stared at the water and kept asking myself: 'God, dear God, how could anyone survive this?'

When the words dried on Gigi's cracked lips and only her body was left to wrestle with the angel of death, the family sent me off on a sightseeing trip. After an unaccountably long train journey, of which all I recall is that everything was flat and grey, I ended up at the home of a friend from my youth, Ági, who had once lived in a two-room partitioned flat on a dull housing estate and used to be one of the best teachers of Hungarian literature in town. In Australia she had become a happy mother of four, lived in a bright, spacious house with a large garden, and was at that time learning to grow medicinal herbs. Books of poetry were piled on the bedside table. We looked around the garden, admired the horses, then took a stroll in the village, down the paths squeezed between the large, clean, bright estates where everyone greeted us with a cheery good day.

On my second day the rain came. It poured and it poured as if it intended to go on for ever. The children blew off to school while we tramped the fields in rubber boots and heavy waterproof coats watching the water rise, inexorably, it seemed. By the third day the roads were impassable and the estate was cut off from the outside world. There was something comically surreal about sitting enveloped in all that wetness at the other end of the Earth where even the stars were back to front – or might have been had we been able to see them – in a place so remote that I kept forgetting its name, while talking about what happened in Budapest in the summer of 1973. That was when Ági left the country in which we grew up and where, I thought, everyone felt at home.

The next day the pavements disappeared. Now we could only walk on the tops of the banks. When we turned off where the end of the last vegetable garden should have been we found an elderly farmer on the slippery side of the incline. So this was what the local peasants looked like, I told myself.

'Look over there, there it is!' the farmer cried and pointed to the black water swirling at the bottom of the slope. I didn't understand what he was telling us, having been struggling with Australian pronunciation this last two weeks. My friend cried out excitedly.

'Yes, yes! There! I see it! I've never seen one in the wild.'

'Me neither, though I've been working the land for years,' the man replied.

I carefully slid down the slope a little way and, once they explained what I was looking for, I finally caught sight of it. A duck-billed platypus was swimming round and round. It was as if now, just as the Earth was preparing to sink into that cold, bubbling water, something had risen out of the deep well of years like a silent invitation to return to the swirling dark ancestral matter where the major issues of creation had not yet been settled, to work its humble way back to a place where no terrible mistakes had yet been made and where anything was possible, where the duck-billed platypus was not one of evolution's blind alleys but a promising line of development that, had we followed it, might have led not to this ever bleaker, ever less forgiving world but to another, more hopeful place. While I was lost in these thoughts, watching the water, Ági and the farmer must have been discussing ways of rescuing the lost creature, because they were bidding each other a cheery goodbye, and then we set out back to the house. Once inside, we put on dry clothes, made a fire, brewed some tea and I was just enjoying the way my multicoloured socks could slide so easily over the wooden floor when the phone rang. Good God, Gigi is dead, I whispered to myself in fright.

The day before the funeral the rain stopped. The military were dropping sandbags from helicopters to make the main roads passable again. My friends made sure I could get on to the first departing train. The route back was bare and grey. Arriving in Sydney I followed instructions and hopped into a taxi, muddy as I was, and sped towards the Jewish cemetery. I arrived to see a tall, bearded man in a hat busily rocking back and forth, singing something.

'How did you manage it?' asked Éva when she embraced me. I shrugged uncomprehendingly and melted into the black mass of mourners.

One morning, almost twenty years after that summer of water and sorrow, I received a letter from Éva. The big padded envelope contained a weathered yellow school notebook containing some poems and diary extracts found after Gigi's death. I opened it carefully then quickly closed it again, and sat for a while in the messy room, clutching the envelope to my breast, full of gratitude and terror. We should have already gone out with the children to make our Wednesday morning visit to the pool, but I sat there on the faded red sofa as if frozen to the spot, staring into space.

'Come here for a moment, kids,' I said eventually.

The children stopped playing with their Lego and sat down next to me. I opened the notebook.

'Can you read this?' I asked.

We started to read slowly, syllable by syllable. We noted how this long dead, ill-fated woman curved her 'k's and looped her capital 'B's and 'E's between the faint guidelines of the book.

> Slow-ly the in-fin-ite days rum-ble past
> Each with its suf-fer-ing worse than the last
> Out there is sum-mer or sun-shine or rain?
> Here, even i-cy cold can't freeze the pain …

Gigi's words of grief were pronounced by my two cheerful, carefree, well-nourished children, as far away from the place to which the memory was attached as they were from the other place where these words were committed to paper, understanding probably less than half of what they read, but reading the words again and again, delighted when they at last made sense of them. At this moment, Gigi stepped out of the mists of mortality and walked back into our lives. For here were two children, blood of her blood, who could recite her words perfectly.

☙

It was hard to sleep in the madness of the days preceding the operation. Once night fell and time was no longer crammed with things to do, the shadows of anxiety crept out of hiding. One sleepless night I was looking out from the balcony. I saw the cars parked in the street below, the stray black dog stealing along the pavement, the withering chestnut tree in front of the flat and the sky bright with stars on a mild night. I tried to imagine my father on his creaky iron bed in hospital and wondered what he was thinking. Was he stuffed full of tranquillisers or was he awake, looking over the dark hospital yard trying to guess the future?

As the delicate currents of air drifted around me I recalled a sleepy Sunday afternoon, I couldn't remember quite where, but in a Mediterranean city somewhere. I was wandering the empty streets as usual when I heard someone playing the '*Internationale*' on a cracked trumpet behind half-closed windows. The tune crept into my ear with a sad, ironic nostalgia. How often had my father sung it happily at a May Day parade, accompanied by hearty colleagues, while our small, dedicated group pounded our way down Népköztársaság Road and Váci Street clutching the red flags lent to us by the union, bellowing, 'The worker's fist is made of steel/It deals the blows it has to deal!' At which my father's eyes would sparkle with pride, even though Váci Street was quite deserted and did not look as though it was trembling at the thought of our iron fists. Only the few foreign tourists we passed looked up in panic: 'What's going on here? We thought demonstrations were banned under the communist dictatorship!'

It was on one of those sleepless July nights before my father died that it first occurred to me how anachronistic those strident May Day parades already were by the middle of the 1960s, and how well they symbolised my father's relationship with time. My father lived in his own time capsule. He was habitually late, not only because he was slow and obstinately preferred to stick to every detail of his normal routine, from the ritual washing to the stuffing full of his briefcase, but because he never wanted to acknowledge that there were other perfectly scientific ways beyond his own subjective method of apportioning time. According to one blood-curdling anecdote, even on 19 March 1944, the day the Germans occupied Hungary, he was still trying to raise subscriptions for *Népszava*, the trade union paper, instead of saving his skin, and he paid no attention at all to the startled, aghast, outraged expressions that greeted his efforts. My father did not want to get old, not just because he feared death but because he felt that the great mission of ensuring that humanity was on the right road still lay before him. It was no use Great Uncle Reality sending him his most faithful maidservant, Time; my father would not admit the uninvited visitor into his house.

I returned to my room and tried to sleep. Thoughts of things to do the next day, of the kind of night my father must have spent, and the next chapter of his book kept going round my head. I couldn't get over that bloody manuscript. It was as if I were afraid that, by constantly missing the point, he was losing his unique last chance, that his fate was being sealed for ever. But after all, I reassured myself, growing steadily sleepier, there is nothing unusual in this. As people age, they often tend to return to the faith of their ancestors. That was his lot. If we could find the cassette player, he could carry on working in the morning and we'd progress faster. And if Dr Cserjés wears a blue tie tomorrow then my father will survive, I heard a spell cross my mind before falling asleep.

Only years after my father's death did it occur to me to think again about the '*Internationale*'. The fifth line says:'Let's wipe the slate clean of the past'. Might we all be victims of a gross semantic misunderstanding, like Michelangelo's Moses with his horns? Was the future delayed by several decades because our wise leaders, as is their wont, were taking the 'Internationale' literally and wanted to clear away the past with bulldozers, hammers and fists of iron?

☙

My maternal grandfather worked as coach-driver for the local landowner. He had a deep contempt for manual labour and avoided school at all costs. He did, however, understand horses, could talk to the gentry, and loved sitting in the driver's seat in his big shiny boots. Beside horses and drink he had another passion: the ruining of tender-hearted maidens. Having filched from the poor girls their one valuable possession, he quickly moved on to seek new prey. And that might have been all right if he had confined himself to seducing only young women of his own class, but my insatiable grandfather was not averse to picking flowers from the gardens of gentlefolk, too. This was roughly at the time when, according to the terms of the first Vienna Award of 1938, Hungary re-pocketed the Northern Hungarian Highlands, in what is now Slovakia, and my grandfather's seed was affectionately stowed not only in my grandmother's and her sister's gardens but also in that of his landowning employer's daughter. When the situation came to light, the indignant representative of the landowning classes, instead of delighting in the potential increase to the Hungarian nation, grabbed a hunting rifle and set out to address the disgrace. My pregnant grandmother was working in the kitchen when she heard the squire bellowing in the dining room about how he was going to shoot the scoundrel like the dog he was. Grandmother leapt through the kitchen window and rushed in panic to the stables to warn Grandfather of the danger. Grandfather made his escape in time while the squire took out his fury on the horses, promising to take care that Grandfather would never be allowed to come near any respectable house in the whole of Szabolcs-Szatmár County. And that was the end of my grandfather's brilliant career, the consequence of which was, naturally, borne by my grandmother and the four bonny children already running round the yard.

The family was driven out to Bokor, a farmstead outside the village, where a wealthy peasant was prepared to shelter them in a small room attached to the stable, in exchange for Grandfather taking care of the horses. It was from here that my mother would set out barefoot to the primary school in the village, and after school, as the family's main breadwinner, to work as a cleaner. My grandfather became even more insufferable, if such a thing were possible. Leaving aside the fact that he was obliged to share one room smelling of horse shit with his entire family, there was not even a woman on the horizon. He'd go into the village to drink, generally when he knew the gentry were absent, and when he returned, his belt tight around his waist, he used his brilliantly polished black boots to kick the youngest child who was sitting on her potty under the table or to slash around with a whip at the rest of them. This untenable situation was brought to an end when Hungary, the ever more ardent and insatiable ally of Hitler's Germany, occupied Sub-Carpathian Ruthenia. In order to ensure the continuity of imperial politics and to disempower the Czechs, to whom the region had previously belonged and who were considered unreliable, the government offered a great number of official posts to Hungarian citizens in the newly reoccupied zone. It was in his regular hangout, the inn of Jóska Balog, that my grandfather was informed that a Hungarian could live like a gentleman among Ruthenians. With the help of his drinking companions he scraped together an application for the post of 'imperial highway cleaner'. A state position! Steady wages! Bicycle provided! A black uniform with braided insignia! For the first time in his life, my grandfather, who was not the dreamy sort, found himself in dreamland. In the few weeks that he waited for an answer, even his domestic violence abated and the village lilies could sway untroubled in the breeze. It was as if ambition – or, to put it more kindly, the hope of a better life – could overcome his natural bloodlust.

Eventually, when he could no longer bear to wait, he strolled over to the local council offices to enquire about the fate of his application. With his big shiny boots and his cap screwed up in his hand, he hung about in the corridor until an official took pity on him and sent him to the right room. Behind a heavy oak desk piled high with documents and files sat a clerk with whey-coloured eyes, his hair licked down, his elbows leather-patched. Grandfather cleared his throat and gave a cautious cough as he did whenever he was in the presence of those of higher social status. On his third try the clerk raised his head and fixed his whey-coloured eyes on Grandfather.

'What do you want?' he barked.

'I've come about my application,' stammered Grandfather.

'What's your name?'

'András Herceg.'

The whey-eyed clerk immersed himself in his work again. It was an eternity before he pulled a sheet of paper from the vast pile on the left-hand side of the desk. Grandfather's heart was beating as he spotted the masterpiece they had concocted in the inn.

'András Herceg?' the clerk barked again, looking my grandfather up and down.

'Yes, sir.'

'Rejected,' the clerk replied and threw the paper back on the top of the pile, his licked hair glimmering.

'Rejected? But why?' whispered my grandfather, white as a sheet.

The clerk didn't even look at him, but since Grandfather continued standing there he eventually picked up the sheet of paper again, clearly nauseated by it, as if it were a toad he was holding. He ran his eye over the notes scrawled on it, then said:

'Because your wife is a non-Aryan.'

According to the Second Jewish Law, passed in

1939, people applying to do state work had to be able to demonstrate two generations back that their ancestors were of pure blood. My grandmother was nothing like the rest of her family: her hair was strawberry blond, her skin freckled and white as milk. Village gossip had it that her mother was an illegitimate Jewish child who, in order to avoid disgrace to her family, had been placed in a home for foundlings, and that Grandmother herself was the illegitimate daughter of a Jewish landlord with whom her mother had been in service in a neighbouring village. What is certain is that when the documents were checked my grandfather could not produce a single christening certificate relating to his wife's family.

'Of course she's Hungarian,' my grandfather replied, emboldened. 'Both her parents were Hungarian. There must be some mistake here, sir.'

'She may be Hungarian but she is not Aryan. You have to have proper proof,' the superior man with the slicked hair replied.

The air froze in silence. A fly kept banging against the window pane again and again as if it couldn't comprehend the fact that there was no escape.

'What does it mean, "Aryan"?' spluttered grandfather eventually. Little streams of sweat were running down the back of his strong, sun-tanned neck.

'It means not Jewish, you idiot. Now get out of here. I'm busy.'

Grandfather made his way home as though he'd got dead drunk at Jóska Balog's inn. Back home my grandmother was in the front yard hanging out to dry the ragged slips of cloth that served as the youngest boy's nappy. When the children spotted their father approaching over the ploughed fields, they dashed into the back yard. The way he walked meant trouble, they could tell. Without a word, my grandfather pushed my grandmother into the room, swayed in after her and collapsed on a chair. He was so angry he couldn't even get the words out. Then, with heavy steps, he strode out into the yard, took the rope used for raising the bucket from the well, carefully wound it round his fist, came back in with it and started to hit my grandmother. She hung on to the remaining scraps of cloth in her hand as tightly as she could. When she eventually fell to the ground Grandfather found his voice at last.

'Jewish whore! Jewish whore!' he kept bellowing in rhythm. Each syllable was accompanied by a blow. Through the window the petrified children watched as their father went about trying to kill their mother. When he was finally exhausted he sunk to the chair and, gasping, let the rope slip from his hand. He wiped the beads of sweat from his brow, gave Grandmother one last hearty kick and set off back to Jóska Balog's inn to rest.

Once she came round from her blood-soaked state, my grandmother opened her fingers, which seemed to have been stuck together, and slowly let the damp rags slide to the ground. It was the first time in her life she wasn't in a hurry. And the first time she felt she had had enough. Her parents had brought her up from the cradle to believe that one must put up with whatever life offers because only the incense-smelling God that lives in the Greek Orthodox church has any say in human affairs. But as she lay beaten on the floor, her bones aching, my grandmother thought she had gone as far as she could. She was no longer ready to get up in the morning, her every muscle tense, and toil day and night in a smoky room, in the fields, at the master's house, beside her husband who rolled on top of her, smelling of *pálinka*, even as the still-suckling infant bellowed in the corner of the room, for no other reason than that more, ever hungry and insatiable infants should be born into this world, to join the other recent lives equally fit for a beating. She had had enough of charring, of hunger; of endless work, work, work, without a break and with no product; of trudging barefoot through muddy fields, of the all-enveloping damp smell of poverty where the sun never shines. As she lay on the cool floor and half-opened her swollen eyes, she saw a strange light glimmering through the small dirty window. The thought that this might spell the end of everything filled her with an unfamiliar lightness of being. Nothing mattered any more, not even the five hungry pairs of eyes staring at her through the glass. It was as if she were already elsewhere, somewhere where there was no love, no responsibility, no pain and no fear. For the first time in her life my grandmother felt she was a full citizen of the empire of infinite freedom beyond the window: she was the mistress of her own fate. She struggled, groaning, to her feet and dragged herself over to the chair where her husband had left the rope. With slow, firm movements, moaning occasionally with pain, she took the rope, threw it over the inner roof beam and made a knot. The children huddled together to watch.

'Is she going to have a swing?' wondered little Mihály jealously.

He had seen swings with white-skirted young women rising and falling against the sky behind the gates of the landlord's garden, when my mother took him along with her when she went cleaning. My not-quite-ten-year-old mother suspected that what her mother was doing was not about swings, but she could not move for terror. Mrs Fehér, the farmer's wife, was just returning from the grocer's when she noticed the Herceg children all crowded round the stable window. When she looked in she clapped her hands and rushed, like a lunatic, for the shears.

You never know in this life who is likely to present you with a gift. While my other two grandparents, for whom I had always longed in vain, allowed history to cast them out of my life, my spiteful, dumb grandfather made it possible for me to scribble these lines in solitude in Geneva. For it was thanks to his desire for a uniform that my mother did not end up in the ovens or in a roadside ditch. I have no idea how the desire for a black uniform with braided insignia got hold of him. As far as I know, state-employed street cleaners did not wear uniform in the occupied territories. But the desire in itself was enough to ensure that at the most critical stage of the war the family moved to the Sub-Carpathians.

My grandfather had never forgiven my grandmother for his having been forced into marriage with her. In his youth, when he seduced her in his usual fashion, it never entered his mind to marry the desperately poor servant girl with her dubious background. He must have believed that being in the service of gentry meant he would meet a better class of peasant girl and finally set one foot on the ladder of social betterment. His ambitions were shattered, however, by the landlord for whom he worked as a coach-driver and my grandmother as a housemaid. When the master noticed that hard-working little Juliska's lovely slender waist had thickened, he bellowed at her until she confessed who was responsible. At which point he summoned my grandfather and ordered him to marry her. Grandfather did not dare disobey the master. And that is how my mother was afforded a couple of months later, the blessed circumstances of a marriage sanctioned by both God and society.

I don't know if the gossip circulating in the village about Grandmother's dubious family background would have been enough to expedite the process of deportation, but who knows what might have happened if they had stayed in Hungary? With what we know of his character and political sympathies, Grandfather would certainly have joined the fascist Arrow Cross. But even if he had avoided the quagmire of politics, the war years' dehumanising turmoil would not have been kind to his dependants. But now that his application had got him into serious trouble, Grandfather felt obliged to do something about his wife. Once he had sobered up, his contacts at the inn soon directed him to the local registrar of births and deaths, who, for a certain consideration, was prepared to line his pockets by modifying the records and producing the necessary documents. A couple of weeks later my grandfather packed the family's entire belongings on to a cheap open cart and set out on the long eastward journey.

Thanks to the complex windings of fate, both my mother and my father, whose families lived in neighbouring villages in Szabolcs-Szatmár County, found themselves in Czechoslovakia in the 1930s. Their routes differed, of course: my father's family fled there to find refuge in an ever more threatened liberal democracy, while my grandfather arrived as conqueror, to play his part as best he could in the destruction of the very same liberal democracy. In the end there was to be no braided black uniform but, up to the arrival of the Red Army in the autumn of 1944, he was proud to wear the tin badge of pre-First World War Hungary sewn to his cap, showing its four rivers (the Danube, the Tisza, the Drava and the Sava) and heraldic three peaks (the Tatra, Matra and Fatra). On her first trip abroad my mother too had some undoubtedly important experiences. For the first time she saw something of the world beyond the mud-caked poverty of her birthplace. She saw the once-affluent towns of Ungvár (Uzhgorod), Munkács (Mukachevo) and Nagyszőlős (Vynohradiv) where now and then she could catch the last sparkling splinter of light of their multi-ethnic pasts. She learned Ruthenian, went to a different kind of school and saw how it was possible to live differently. And what was most important, she witnessed how her best friends, the two pigtailed Frankel sisters, were driven on to cattle wagons. But she didn't have to stumble on with them.

Long before I ever asked my mother why her father kept shouting, 'Jewish whore!' as he beat my grandmother, we were always teasing her that she was a real Yiddishe momme, because every morning she ate matzos for breakfast, never found the objects of our love quite good enough for us, and wasn't satisfied until she managed to nag the best possible qualifications out of us. She went with her best friend to visit Israel and was received there like a native; she wept her way through reams of Holocaust literature and made better poppyseed and apple cake than anyone could buy from the famous Fröhlich pattiseries. But I am sure that not for one moment did she ever stop to consider whether all this was 'Jewish' or not. It wasn't a relevant question for her. For my mother, being determined consciousness, as she learned once and for ever at a Marxist-Leninist mind-broadening seminar. To be more precise about this, what she learned there confirmed what she already knew. It is quite certain that her consciousness was formed by the unambiguous lessons of the conditions under which she grew up, that is to say servant-class poverty, although her ancestors on her mother's side were likely to have been of Jewish origin. In her childhood it was the basic language of poverty she spoke, in which the only matter of importance was the short-term justice of your next meal. What proportion of my mother's complex being is down to individual character, childhood experience or unknown genetic heritage, it is impossible to say and it is not even interesting. We cannot know how she came by her great generous spirit, her thirst for knowledge and her gift of laughter, but we are infinitely grateful for all of them.

How far being determines consciousness, which being does the determining, or indeed whether it is the other way round – that consciousness produces being – naturally, such details did not disturb the quick-fix seminar's successful gallop to the Great Truths. Though it was by no means a simple matter, even in my parents' personal lives. When my mother, at the age of sixteen, arrived at her first Party school, she couldn't tell the time from a clock, didn't know how to eat with a knife and fork and had never slept in her own bed on her own sheets. Beside the essential concepts of Marxism-Leninism-Stalinism she also had to learn the basics of everyday civilised existence, and learn them so impossibly fast that no one would notice. Her studies proved so successful that in the next fifty years that she spent with my father, who by then managed to wipe away all memory of genteel behaviour, she could trade banter with him, enquiring of him with a happy maternal smile: 'Let's see now, which of us had a proper upbringing with a room of one's own?'

The second minor point concerning consciousness-determined being is that people are conditioned not only by circumstances of which sometimes there is no outward sign at all, but by the stuff out of which they are made. My mother's family on both sides came from the lowest depths of rural poverty. But while misery on her mother's side led to a desperate clinging together, her father's branch were like hungry wolves and lost no opportunity to go for one another's throats. My mother's maternal grandfather was a day labourer on a tobacco farm. At weekends, when he went to visit his grandchildren, he'd climb the roadside white mulberry tree and fill his cap so he might surprise them with a little gift. If he found no wild fruit he'd bring his zither and play music for them so they might forget their hunger. Mother's grandparents were 'in love': an expression my mother first heard when neighbours were discussing how her grandmother, who was twenty years younger than her husband, died soon after him, of grief.

Meanwhile, on her father's side it was all ruthlessness, hatred, bad blood and rampant pride. When the family returned home after the war, they were greeted along the street by the sight of the corpse of one of her uncles, frozen in blood. The villagers whispered that he had lost his wife at cards with some of the liberating Soviet troops and because she was unwilling to go with them, they stabbed him. According to another version he was the victim of a simple bar-room brawl. What is, however, certain is that my mother's favourite brother, five-year-old Jancsi, died of diphtheria because Grandfather's brother wouldn't allow them to use his cart to take the child to the doctor. Uncle Gyurka became a relatively wealthy peasant by forcing his own parents and brothers into service. He wouldn't lend the cart because they couldn't pay his expenses. It was no use little Jancsi screaming out in fever: 'I don't want to die! I don't want to die!' Uncle Gyurka remained unmoved. My mother stopped her ears and ran to the neighbouring village for some medicine. In their own village the doctor and the dispensing chemist, both of whom were Jewish, had been taken away. By the time she returned, her legs scratched and sore, with the medicine clutched in her sweaty hands, my grandmother was already out in the courtyard repeatedly bowing over the dead child. For years my mother kept hearing his screams. When it came to dividing up the land, when people were forced into collectives, and when the legal system was overhauled 'in the name of the people', my mother felt she knew exactly what it was all about. Not to mention the fact that when any child in the family developed a fever, we were immediately rushed off to the doctor.

My grandmother spent her entire life paying off the debt she owed, on account of her one act of rebellion: defying the incense-scented Greek Orthodox God she had been brought up to love by her parents of such dubious extraction. She was convinced that that was why her youngest child contracted diphtheria and died, why her second daughter gave birth to doomed Siamese twins joined at the head, why her thirty-year-old son died of a heart attack while getting off a long-distance bus, why one of her sons ended up a convict, and why all her children bar one became God-denying pagans. She dressed in black from the moment of her convalescence to the day she died, hoping in this way to forestall any further potential disasters. But despite serving such a harsh life sentence, she was never bitter. Her hands, which were lined with veins thick as tree roots, could produce an endless succession of gorgeous flowers, a thriving vegetable garden, plump doughnuts, suckling pigs and darned socks. She spent every winter at our Németvölgyi Road flat so she wouldn't have to put up with the cold back in her village. I don't think she understood much of what her feather-brained Pest granddaughters were blabbering at her. Once, after much rehearsal, we sang her a social realist hit song of the time, 'Dear Grandma'. She listened through to the end, a little embarrassed, then quickly went out into the kitchen to get on with some work. At the time of the folk-song revival of the 1970s, led by

Ferenc Sebő, we tried to preserve something of her store of folk tunes on a tape recorder, but she could only remember some church hymns, intoning them in a thin, reedy voice. We were always begging her to take off her black headscarf so that we might see her long, braided pigtail. She would wave us away in irritation but always gave in eventually. We touched with an almost religious awe the tender white skin under her headscarf, so strangely different from the sunburned and lined skin on her normally visible face. It was as if she were revealing, just for a moment, her secret inner being, one never before seen by anyone else, one that had preserved her untouchable purity.

Every step Grandmother took was accompanied by a barely audible creak because she squeezed her bunion-lined feet into high-laced shoes so they wouldn't hurt so much. It was the first sound I heard when she entered our room on those still dark winter dawns. Every morning she prepared egg yolk stiffened with sugar so that our days would be sweet and in the evenings she would carefully polish our scuffed shoes so we might be fittingly dressed the following day for the house of learning. Not that the house of learning wrought any particular sense of awe in her, but she respected our family's peculiar notions. She loved my father as though he were her long-lost son and when, ten or so years after my parents were married, she noticed that he was left-handed, she made sure to pray that it should not lead him into trouble. She lived in a world of ancient beliefs, home soil and sheer instinct, ever fearful because the wrath of God might strike her at any time. She rejoiced when it failed to strike. She regarded every freshly appearing seedling, every new chick, anything she managed to cultivate, anything at all that grew that was not beaten down by hail or rain or war, every child that was spared, as a gift. Her generosity knew no bounds because she wanted to show how thankful she was for all these blessings. Her arms and legs were full of knots, her heart was gold and her gaze, even at the age of eighty-five, was as clear as a cloudless sky.

The summer she died I was barely capable of weeping for her because I'd spent all my tears on another death. At the beginning of that summer my friend Vera had taken the pills that had killed her. I travelled down to the village for my grandmother's funeral, then returned to Budapest, packed and set off to the other side of the world. Years later, travelling on the number six tram, I noticed another hand just as full of knots as my grandmother's. I got off, turned down the first side street I came to and hurried on to my business. It was only some minutes later, when I sank down on my haunches to pick up the important documents I had dropped, that I noticed I was crying. There would never again be hands like my grandmother's hands.

One day when I came home from school, I found my grandmother doubled up on a kitchen chair.

'What's the matter, Grandmother? Are you ill?' I asked.

She wouldn't say. Seemingly relieved that now someone was home, she hastened about her tasks again. That made me think she was not ill. She hadn't turned on the light because she was by herself and it cost money. After a while, as she was polishing something, she stiffened again. She gave me an anxious look, then asked warily:

'What's that noise?'

'What noise?' I asked.

'That noise, now.'

'I can't hear anything,' I answered reassuringly.

It was only after some time had passed and she asked again that I realised it was the noise of the lift that frightened her.

'It's just the lift, Grandmother,' I said with all the assurance of an enlightened city dweller. 'You know, the motor that drives the lift up and down.'

A faint smile of relief passed across her face. I saw she was not entirely convinced, but she drew herself up and started working again. It was only when I recalled the incident decades later that I thought more deeply about it and wondered what memories of terror and exploitation had suddenly surfaced, producing in her something monstrous enough to stop her working, she who never stopped working. I saw her crouched in the corner of the kitchen, a tiny thing, and imagined how great the ancient terror of fire, of storms, of lightning, of all unknown things must have been and how the unpredictable God had constantly to be appeased with handsome gifts. What was worse, I asked myself, the terror of unknown or of known evil?

Even now I can't answer that question, but I do remember not laughing at my grandmother then. Despite having all the assurance of an urban elementary school girl, I knew exactly what terror had her by the throat. I had exactly the same howling and trembling animal fear of death. Like my grandmother, I would sit in my room after the lights were switched off, hearing my parents in the next room whispering about the latest political developments, and fix my eyes on the thin line of light under the door and consider how I might avoid death. My parents were of no help in solving that question. My mother stood firm on dialectical materialism, but everything she said only worried me more. My father was unwilling even to discuss the subject. Naturally, never a word was passed about what had happened to him and his family in the war, but neither did he discuss the plane crash at the beginning of the 1960s in which several of his best friends died or, some time later, the suicide of this or that friend or comrade-in-arms. When I mentioned my doubts to my sister her mocking answer was:

'How do you imagine we'd squeeze into this country if everyone from the time of our founder Great King Árpád were still here cluttering up the place?'

There was no answer to that. I listened to my sister snuffling in her sleep while I lay in despair in my bed trying to come to terms with the powers of the darkness.

'Long live Kennedy!' I whispered, my throat dry.

I hoped that my colossal betrayal might wring some pity from the lords of the dark heavens so they might send me to the alternative queue. I couldn't quite explain to myself why the tyrants of imperialism and their lackeys should be in the realm of the immortals, but that didn't matter. For a couple of days after my betrayal my conscience racked me dreadfully. It was perfectly true that no one knew about it and that the sky didn't fall in, but I was still very troubled. Furthermore, another depressing thought quickly came to mind. Why, after all, should I be the one spared rather than, say, the great poet Endre Ady? Taking everything into account, he was far more deserving of immortality than I was. Yet still he died. That's no answer. Furthermore, John F. Kennedy was brutally assassinated a little later, so I was forced to admit he was not immune from the great reckoning. My inner demons continued to torment me. And so it went on until two or more years later, one Friday afternoon, just as I was leaping down the stairs in the glazed stairwell of my friend Juli's sixth-floor flat, it occurred to me that if we lived for ever then nothing mattered. Then it's all the same. This idea seemed such a revelation I immediately had to share it with somebody. Although Juli was probably my best friend, I had never discussed metaphysics with her. Not to mention the fact that in order to do so I'd have to climb right back up to the sixth floor again. So I rushed home, but there was nobody there. I hunted feverishly through my chest of drawers for some written testimony to my epoch-making discovery. Soon enough I came across these lines by the Transylvanian poet Domokos Szilágyi:

> Good morning – and a lovely death;
> A summer it's worth dying for,
> A summer after which death comes easy.

I immediately copied the lines on to a clean piece of white card and pinned it above my bed so that when I felt the anxiety again, I would have them there to remind me. My father did not think the quotation quite concrete enough (summer could not be readily identified with the class struggle), my mother thought it too morbid and my sister had had enough of quotations pinned above my bed. But the card remained there for years, even after I discovered that the writer of those lines committed suicide.

In 1944, when the Red Army began its unstoppable push west and had reached the foot of the Carpathians, the soldiers carried off every male of Hungarian descent for some *malenky robot*, or 'little work' – a euphemism for forced labour in Soviet territories – in my grandfather's case, to the barely concealed relief of his growing infants. Grandmother sent my teenage mother off to try and find him. She didn't succeed but as she was rushing across a ruined railway bridge to escape some low-flying war planes she fell and broke her knee. She was discovered by a young Soviet major who put splints around her swollen leg and helped her hobble home. The next evening, before the troops marched on, the major returned to the road mender's cottage to bring my mother some pills to soothe her fever. It was hard for my mother to find the right words to thank him. For the first time in her life, here was someone who thought it mattered what happened to her.

It was only in the late 1950s that my grandfather finally found himself back home after *malenky robot*: long years spent in the Gulag and in the village to which he returned after he had been released and which he could not leave since in the meantime he had become a Soviet citizen. We don't know what happened to him in his long absence. He never spoke about it and it seems no one asked. All we know is that after a few years of forced labour they let him go and he was allowed to return to his last place of residence in the Carpathian foothills, which had in the meantime become part of the Ukrainian Soviet Socialist Republic. He might have worked in the local co-operative, like everyone else, and certainly could have played some part in the region's demographic recovery.

When the liberalising effects of the Gorbachev period reached the frontiers of the USSR and the authorities gave us permission to travel, my mother, my Uncle Mihály and I paid a visit to the village where they spent those crucial war years. Everything had changed so much as to be unrecognisable. It was as if the pre-war period had vanished into a distant Neolithic past. People seemed to be living in a numbed version of the eternal present. There was only one toothless old woman in a black headscarf who faintly remembered the time when Jews, Roma and Hungarians all lived in the neighbourhood, and that among them there was one road mender from Szabolcs-Szatmár County with his extensive family.

In the spring of 1957 when, thanks to the milder political climate under Khrushchev, my grandfather was able to leave the Soviet Union at last and return to his birthplace, he picked up exactly where he had left off. The house had stood empty and locked, though the evidence of my grandmother's work was visible in the garden. My grandfather was enraged when he discovered that his wife had learned to read, had signed on to the local co-operative and at this moment happened to be in Budapest on a visit. His ungrateful children had not only taken possession of his treasured bicycle but had moved away, learned trades, set up families without his permission and, what's more, his bastard daughter (my mother) had married a stinking Jew.

When, after suppressing the 1956 uprising, the government re-established order and the railway service was restored, my grandmother went home to see her husband after more than a decade of absence. A couple of months later we received a letter from the neighbours warning us that if we did not intervene my grandfather would beat my grandmother to death. My two uncles, Mihály and István, who were grown-up by then, went over to the village with a solemn vow to pay their father back once and for all. They had almost kicked the life out of him when my grandmother threw herself between him and them and begged them to have mercy. Grandfather never again raised a hand against her, but drank himself quietly into terminal cancer and, twenty years later, coughed his life out in her arms. Whenever we visited them – very rare occasions – he'd waste no time necking the bottles we brought as presents and hung about the tiny yard in front of the house with a dreamy smile, muttering through a throat that had undergone surgery: 'The smaller the house the greater the happiness.'

Fourth

My father, the stinking Jew, never suspected what a storm he had caused in the shallows of his father-in-law's soul. He was spending his week's holiday at one of the Party's Lake Balaton resorts along with a teacher colleague and a group of outstandingly able students. Naturally he continued his strenuous efforts to educate them. However, when the time came that there were no more seminars, no more work to mark, not one comrade to be affirmed in his faith, he walked and walked the dark streets so he shouldn't be left alone in his room to confront the vacuum in his soul.

One hot, balmy evening, he was pounding the streets of the resort, hurrying past the lit garden restaurants so no one would recognise him. But as he was passing one of them he heard ringing laughter. He hardly noticed as an invisible force carried him up the worn steps and deposited him at a table by himself, opposite the noisy young crowd. He watched them in some confusion but with satisfaction. It was a group of first-year students, the hope for the future in whom he, among others, had nursed the seed of faith. He didn't understand much of their loud conversation and jokes because all his attention was fixed on the beautiful creature with sparkling green eyes who, he thought, was the source of that ringing laughter. He was right. A couple of minutes later one of the young men made a remark that brought on a fresh bout of cackling. The brown-haired girl was laughing with her head thrown back and in her wild movement she upset the glass of cheap brandy in front of her. But she thought this was so funny that her peals of laughter reached a new bright pitch, rising ever higher. Her unselfconscious laugh filled my father with such unknown happiness that, for a moment, he forgot the clumsy language of the Party and his own uncultured directness and, with a gallant gesture that he must have observed in his father at some Prague café, he stood up, bowed in front of my mother and said: 'Let me order you a fresh glass!'

My mother looked up, her eyes still wet with laughter, and met the gaze of what seemed to her a dark-eyed little boy.

'What lovely black hair he has!' she thought.

The next moment she realised that the gallant gentleman standing in front of her was none other than Comrade Holló, her lecturer in Marxism. She was so embarrassed that she blushed from ear to ear, which only made her appear more beautiful. She turned back to her companions without a word. But she accepted the watered-down sherry brandy and sipped awkwardly at it for what remained of the evening, as if she felt that this love potion might have life-long effects.

With his first and possibly only gesture of gallantry my father won the jackpot, my mother's hand. My mother who, through her contacts with Party education at various institutions, had started getting used to being thought of as a person in her own right, felt with all her unerring female instincts that the clumsy youth teaching her the principles of Marxism-Leninism did not regard her quite as his colleagues did when they delightedly marked the progress of this poor peasant creature, watching the effects of the drip-drip of knowledge on her flowering consciousness. Returning to the Party school in Budapest, she couldn't help but notice that that warm brown gaze was following her everywhere. It was not coincidence, was it, that she kept bumping into Comrade Holló at the most unexpected moments, whether in school or out of it? It was as if the young tutor knew her precise weekly timetable, as well as the times of the main-line trains to Nyíregyháza on which she travelled once a month to visit her relatives. And, despite all her natural shyness, my mother might have admitted to herself that she instinctively looked for that abundant dark head of hair whenever she was on the move. A couple of months later she was prepared to walk out with the owner of that head of hair and was enthusiastically joining in discussions with him on the education of the rural proletariat.

And it might have remained thus, and my mother might have returned at the end of her course of study to Szabolcs-Szatmár County to help build up the young national democracy, had not fate stepped in in the modest figure of Comrade Kovács, the local Party secretary. One sunny May afternoon Comrade Kovács called the trainee cadre with the long pigtail and sparkling eyes into his office to discuss the bright future that lay before her.

'You know, comrade,' said Kovács, leaning forward unexpectedly, 'a highly promising young cadre like you shouldn't be spending time with a Jew.'

My mother went as red as the flag of the 'Internationale'. She didn't immediately realise what Comrade Kovács was talking about. But she recognised the sick feeling at the pit of her stomach. She felt the same terror mixed with shame that had gripped her every time she saw her father at the end of the path, his belt tightly buckled. Or when she had seen her closest friends, the Frankel sisters, being marched up the middle of the road with yellow stars over their hearts. Suddenly an invisible fence had divided her from them and my child mother had known that terrible things would happen on the other side of that fence. She had stepped out of the staring crowd to slip a piece of bread into their hands, but the soldier guarding them had pushed her away with the butt of his rifle.

'I'm afraid your warning comes a little late, Comrade Kovács,' she replied boldly. 'We're getting married tomorrow afternoon.'

She rushed straight from Comrade Kovacs's office to my father's room.

'Get ready. We're getting married,' she announced in a voice that would brook no argument.

My poor father gasped in surprise at having the secret object of his desire drop into his lap like that, without any notice. He could only mumble in confusion that he had a class the next afternoon, and that he lacked a suit. My mother with her aforementioned unerring feminine instinct knew that now their lives were conjoined she'd have to arrange everything. She found a suit, some witnesses and someone to sit in for his class and the next day, a mild afternoon in May 1952, before the XIIIth District comrade registrar they settled their lives by stuttering the appropriate vows.

Not counting the golden years of Prague, the next few cloudless months he spent with my mother in a single room sublet in Visegrádi Street were probably the happiest of my father's life. It's true that she kicked up no end of a fuss when on the first of the month he turned up with a sackful of books rather than his pay, but she quickly calmed down and soon enough they were rolling with laughter on the narrow bed. Then, little by little, her siblings from the village moved up to Budapest and my mother settled them in various schools so they might escape the lives of poverty they had been fated to live so far. Some self-destructive urge had led them all to leave education early, something they regretted only decades later. Even the partners they chose ensured that their childhood nightmares would never be over. The girls married handsome, violent drunks, the boys married pretty, servile women and after a few decades they regretted that, too. It was as if only my mother had inherited the curiosity, resilience and furious desire for change that must have built up over the generations. But the various family members remained in the Visegrádi Street sublet until their fates were settled, usually for the worse. In the meantime my parents' own first child arrived and the international situation grew more tense. The father of the nations, our guide Stalin, died and the Soviet Union under Khrushchev seemed nowhere near as solid a fortress as when the aged dictator had it firmly gripped in his iron fist. By the end of October 1956, by which time I was supposed to have been born were it not for the 'regrettable October events', my father had probably forgotten that the purpose of life could be the search for happiness.

Due to the above-mentioned historical events the relationship between my father and myself set off very much on the wrong foot. According to the doctors, I should have been born at the end of October, but in view of the great rebellion I decided to spend a little longer in the comfort of my mother's womb. Nature follows its own sense of order despite the chaos outside. Every day my mother suffered labour pains. Since there was no public transport, despite severe cramps, she was obliged to walk all the way to the Kútvölgyi hospital from the Németvölgyi Road flat into which, after much pleading, my father had consented to move two years before. My father anxiously gripped my mother's arm and tried to cover her enormous belly with his own thin frame. The rebels were firing on the comrades from Kopaszhegy Hill, or it might have been vice versa. Whichever way you looked at it, it was an uncomfortable situation. When they reached the hospital, the revolutionary representative or the Russian doctor, whoever momentarily had the upper hand, took turns to remind my mother loudly that she had chosen a fine time to give birth. It was only in the middle of November, well after the return of the Soviet tanks, that I was finally ready to show my face, by which time there had already been quite enough trouble on my account.

In the meantime the storm of history had swept away all the co-habiting relatives who had faithfully followed my parents into the new flat in Buda. My grandmother was stuck with relatives in a village on the Pest side of the river, my aunt had a cycling accident and was lying unconscious in the János hospital, while my uncle was hiding in a garage because our emboldened neighbours wanted to beat him to death on account of his tan shoes which indicated to them that he was a member of the security police. As to my father, he was on call to protect the alliance of workers and peasants, led by Soviet-supporting Comrade Kádár. My two-and-a-half-year-old sister was left to play by herself in the Németvölgyi Road flat. The neighbours fed her and she always had somewhere to sleep, but who knows what was going on in that clever little head of hers in those two weeks? Whatever it was, for years, whenever she was cross with someone, she didn't call the person an idiot but simply blazed at them: 'You counter-revolutionary!'

Postpartum fever and other associated problems kept my mother in hospital until the beginning of December. She made her way home in flurries of snow with the baby swaddled up against the cold. Back home in the flat she was confronted by her chubby and filthy firstborn, who looked suspiciously at the silent package in her arms. The neighbours were so preoccupied with the dramatic twists and turns of history happening outside that it hadn't occurred to anyone to give my sister a bath. My mother set to getting some hot water and tried explaining to the little girl that her much-anticipated sister had arrived. A few days later my father reappeared having played his part in the defence of the Cause, peeked into the bundle in front of him and declared that my nose was too big.

It may be that the summer my father died really started in the summer of 1956, when one by one a series of terrible truths burst upon him which he did not have the strength to confront. What was more, as a final tribulation, his second child was born at the end of it, the false heir who was neither a boy nor a fit person to tread the path already laid down by him with so much sacrifice. Poor Father!

Decades later, when I came across some strikingly different interpretations of the 1956 events from those I had grown up with, I was astonished to discover that not only my origins but the circumstances of my birth were far from what I had understood them to be. It was not only the yellow star but 1956 that I would carry as a stigma for the rest of my life. Nobody had bothered to inform me that I was too late for history because the very seed of the ideal with which I was to be brought up, that is to say democratic socialism with a human face, had been quite stamped out before I was born. So successfully had it been stamped out that some thirty-one years later, when political change became possible again, socialism with a human face was not even on the agenda. I grew up with an image of 1956 that had been one of a thirst for vengeance, for lynchings, for revisionism and anti-Semitism. It was with shock and shame that I learned that all this was just the scum left behind by the wave. That wave was the conviction of the majority of people that they could no longer live a lie.

And of course no one informed me that my beloved parents were on the side of those who thought 1956 was not a wave at all, just scum.

It's another question that after 1990, under our newly re-established democracy, 1956 became ever more the possession of the scum. By the time the more enlightened members of my parents' generation, such as my mother, came to re-evaluate the events of 1956, gangs of booing and spitting 'freedom fighters' howled down our much-loved president, Árpád Göncz, one of the few genuine heroes of the uprising, when he tried to make a speech at the annual commemoration. Friends of my parents saw this and solemnly wagged their heads as if to say: 'See, we told you so!'

ꕤ

The constant blare of horns and the whine of ambulances racked the heat-drowsy city. But inside the cool green shade of the hospital there were only hushed voices, the sibilance of trolleys, the dull clip-clop of wooden sandals. It was close to silence. It was as if within the shell of the agitated world some calm kernel were secreted, a place where the essential carried on happening. But what kind of 'essential'? My doomed father was shivering with cold: he was still fiddling with the sails of the political windmill. One afternoon when I escaped the noise outside and dropped in on him I found him bent over, sitting on the sagging metal bed, staring in front of him with a vacant expression. In those few seconds before he noticed me his face was a picture of absolute loneliness.

Loneliness is born of lack of trust. My father trusted no one except my mother, who had become so much a part of his life that, after a while, he hardly noticed that she had her own individual existence, that she was someone the merciful deities had assigned to him. After the joy of the first few years of their marriage her presence became natural to him, not a daily gift he had to thank the gods for. He had no trust in his children, and indeed time proved he was right not to trust us, though his distrust predated any such proof. Without trust there can be no love and without love there can be no friendship. It didn't matter how many people he had around him: he remained lonely.

The Soviet system was built only partly on electrification and collectivisation; the rest was distrust. The system snapped the apparently unbreakable bond between people, destroying it root and branch; it deposited people in unfamiliar places, shoved them into a labyrinth of secret reports, betrayals and blackmail until their trust in each other was utterly wrecked. If you didn't know when or why your son, friend, lover or colleague was likely to report you to the authorities, there remained only doubt which ate away your soul. Hamlet doesn't trust anyone: one by one the pillars of his existence crumble and he is left alone at the end staring at nothing. Then that nothing is occupied by a foreign power.

I met the Hamlet who trusts no one in Peter Brook's production, when his company performed in Geneva in late 1998, the autumn before my father died. Hamlet loses everything: only words remain to him, and he tries to solve everything with words, although words are what he least trusts. Nevertheless his last wish is that Horatio should tell his story as though vanishing without trace was more terrifying to him than death itself. I watched the play I knew so well, breathless. Those several-hundred-year-old words of mourning, love, doubt and despair echoed deeply in my own tense body; it was as if I had spoken them myself. In great works of art human memory is conserved so that we don't have to stutter when it is our turn to speak. The sudden nearness of anticipated loss sharpened my senses as I watched Ophelia. Ophelia is liberated through mourning. For the first time in her life she does what she wants and says what she thinks. As if grief … What? Is it possible to mourn Polonius, too?

☙

One afternoon when I was on the metro on my way to the hospital, numbed by the constant daily emotional tension, I was whiling away the time studying the faces of my fellow passengers. Those prematurely aged, uncommunicative faces with their careworn expressions, the women with their painted nails and hairdos, the men with shopping bags quite sunk into themselves, normally filled me with such tenderness and sadness that I felt that, despite almost sixteen years of absence with just the occasional longer or shorter visit, it was the Budapest metro, not Geneva, not London, not California, that was my true home: these were faces that I could read and understand; I knew what lay behind them, or at least I could make a decent guess. But on this hot afternoon when everyone was pushing and shoving, I no longer had the heart for it. I pulled out my newspaper and buried myself in it. At Moszkva Square three gypsy youths and a girl got on. One of the boys sat down beside me and, impudently rubbing his thigh against mine, started reading over my shoulder. I didn't say anything but hung on to the chrome-plated pole next to me, trying to make sense of Dezső Tandori's piece in front of me, a text that swayed in harmony with the movement of the carriage. His poems which, in our youth, had offered us truths that were crystal clear and could cut like a diamond – that is, providing we could understand them – had over the years become an ever-more complex weave of textures. But maybe it was just that I was finding it harder to follow its various strands. Being a faithful reader, though, I was sticking to the task, working at it hard. Somewhere near Kossuth Square the boy spoke.

'Who is Seneca?'

I looked at him in surprise. The title of the piece was 'The Letters of Seneca'.

'An old Greek philosopher.'

'What's a philosopher?'

I tried to explain as best I could.

'And what happened to him?'

'What do you mean, what happened?'

'How did he die?'

'They didn't like him much, because he said what he

thought, and eventually they gave him a glass of poison to drink.'

'And he drank it?'

'He did.'

'Why?'

'To show them he was right.'

At this point I had realised that in my surprise I had confused Seneca with Socrates, but it didn't matter by then.

'Was he a Jew?' the boy asked, after thinking for a while.

'Who?' I replied, slightly on the defensive.

'That Seneca, or whatever his name is?'

'No, there were few Jews at that time. Or rather there were Jews but not like Jews today.' I was growing ever more muddled.

'Was he a gypsy?'

'No. As I said, this happened many centuries ago.'

'But you are still reading his letters?' he asked, impressed.

'That's right,' I said, but looked up and noticed I had missed my stop. When I stood up and he spotted the half-sized guitar case behind me his face lit up.

'Are you a violinist?'

'No, this is a child's guitar and I need to change the strings,' I replied quickly. 'Bye now.'

As the train squealed to a deafening halt, I was for a moment filled with a sharp desire to lean over and stroke his face while he was still looking at me in that puzzled manner. But I managed to pull myself together and push my way through the door. In the crush of other passengers I turned and saw the startled expressions on the faces of the other two boys. Once I reached the surface, I was immediately struck by the strong sunlight, the noise, the heavy smell of summer in the city made up of the stench of exhaust, garbage and perspiring bodies. I stood for a few moments next to the escalator as if debating whether to flee back down the sticky stairs into the drumming darkness. Then I resolved to throw myself into the flow of city traffic. When, towards the end of the afternoon, I reached the hospital, I asked my father about Seneca and about why he wrote the *Consolations*. As will be clear by now, my philosophical education had not extended to him.

I have to get used to this new city, with its beggars searching through the rubbish, through the human wrecks boarding trams, the overwhelming flood of traffic, the characteristic trail of dog shit, the homeless people squatting by the entrances of elegant cafés, the subways turning into jungles haunted by the poor and piles of litter, the potholed pavements silently bearing the marks of hasty workmanship, the noise that follows you everywhere because there is no coffee bar, no supermarket, no newspaper stall that does not avail itself of a TV or a radio loud with continuous jokey banter occasionally interrupted by commercials. I have to decode and re-code new bus routes, not to mention the latest ideas. I have to get used to all those people on the street apparently talking to themselves, not all of them crazy as they were in my childhood; but they talk to someone on their brand new cell-phones, which means they can't be, or don't want to be, wherever they actually are. The elemental, unshakable reality of being 'here and now' is in the process of disintegration. Since it is possible to step out of it at any time, there is nothing that needs to be fully experienced. The playground is no longer a playground because in it the busy parents are chattering and doing deals. The tram is no longer a public place where passengers share space with those who happen to be in the same carriage: people constantly break the conversation, slip out of a theatre, or even duck briefly out of a funeral because of some urgent matter that cannot be postponed. The only problem is that whatever is happening in the conversation, at the theatre or the cemetery loses significance so everything turns into a constant background hum while space and time become ever more amorphous and indefinable. We can no longer tell clearly the difference between external and internal places and events; our life is becoming a grey mass out of which feelings and passions occasionally emerge, then quickly melt back into the dense tide flowing irresistibly towards the Great Funnel down which we are all, without exception, doomed to vanish.

'It's because the universe is speeding up,' declared the saleswoman in the shop, with all the assurance of one who knows she is properly informed. I was buying fruit juice for my father. 'That's why everything is in a mad rush. The planets are accelerating. Matter is going to get ever denser and we'll have a new Big Band. Of course, I'll be long gone by then.'

She practically sang the last words. I nodded enthusiastically. When my countrymen are not at each other's throats, they are busily engaged in conversation: in shops, at the post office, on the street, in front of the phone booth. They still love to chat with strangers and share their preoccupations. There's not much else they are prepared to share, but thoughts, accounts and remarks are still part of the common currency. Perhaps the need to communicate is all that remains of the rich vein of really-existing socialism in what was once the Eastern Bloc: that and a few ill-fitting doors, some dripping taps and those ever-draughty stairwells.

☙

My father's death visibly began in the summer of 1992 at the outbreak of the first Yugoslavian war. It might not be a coincidence that the happy innocent childhood I was lucky enough to enjoy came to an end with my father's death and the break-up of Yugoslavia. Until then, despite all warnings to the contrary, I believed that people were essentially good, that truth would eventually win out, that evil would meet the fate it deserved and that we were all immortal. I thought that while a moral universe founded on solid values might occasionally find itself in conflict with reality, such conflicts could always be resolved. I could, if I so desired, explain away my father's illness and his inevitably approaching death, and that helped me to accept it. It was becoming cruelly apparent that the new world that was just then coming into being was not going to accommodate my father and his beliefs. Looking at it from the other side, I might have added that he had no strength left in him. He had had to survive a great deal in the past and there were ever fewer sources of power he could use to recharge himself. He was always so absorbed in the service of the Cause that he never learned that you could supplement your store of energy with something as simple as a book, an excursion or just enjoying the company of another person.

But that other death that, two hours away from us, was wiping out entire families, streets, villages in such a hurry, that led old schoolfriends, neighbours and former wedding guests to cutting each other's throats in the name of some obscure issue of ethnic belonging – that I couldn't understand. Or, to be more precise, I didn't want to understand. In this I was just like my father who, when confronted with all the negative evidence about really-existing socialism, hastily reviewed the accounts to find some excuse; and so I too refused to accept that the terrible scenes being played out before our terrified gaze by our country's southern neighbours were in fact all true. I must have felt that if I accepted it, my entire world view – starting with my belief in the essential goodness of people through to my faith in the benign wisdom, or at least rational behaviour, of democratically elected governments – was not valid. Then humanity was indeed the sowing of dragon's teeth. Which, in retrospect, also meant that the gas chambers of the Second World War and the initial indifference of Western governments to their existence were not part of a brief historical anomaly, but the norm, the logical result of a certain rationality. In other words, it could happen again at any time.

By the time we reached the seventh year of my father's slow agony that had followed the course of the Yugoslavian bloodbath, I came to believe that anything was possible. Perhaps that is why my determination wavered in the dance around my father's sickbed. However much I resisted the thought, I understood that events were not informed by our values and desires. All through the Yugoslavian horror I was arguing that each drop of blood spilt would be the last and that each act of wickedness would prompt a severe response. When the people of Bosnia voted overwhelmingly for a pluralist multi-ethnic democracy and Karadžić's troops massacred the voters, when they bombed the crowded marketplace at Sarajevo, when they starved, murdered and tortured several thousands of prisoners behind barbed wire, when the barely armed peacekeeping troops allowed the men of Srebrenica to be led off and then piled into mass graves day after day, once I had overcome the shock, I was continually hoping that now at last the world would be sufficiently shaken to recover its conscience and intervene immediately to stop the killing. But the world's conscience did not wake, or in any case it arrived posthumously, once the corpses were buried deep underground; and one weak, overdue flicker only served to generate some guilt.

While I was reluctantly backing out of childhood I was forced to admit that, going by the evidence, it wasn't a desire for 'freedom and love' that made the world go round, and that in order to understand events one had to see them not only from the point of view of the humiliated victim but from the other side, too, because – again going by the evidence – it seemed that that was where events started. On that other side, however, I was horrified to observe that the lust for power was stronger than anything else. In the light of this unpleasant discovery, what happened in peace-time Cambodia, where one in seven of the population was murdered to the sound of socialist slogans, immediately became comprehensible. Not to mention events closer to home.

By the summer of 1992, when snipers were competing to see how many pram-pushing mothers, shaky old grandfathers or children running to fetch water they could hit from their positions in the hills surrounding Sarajevo, my father could barely move for the pain caused by the swelling in his head. By the time they ushered him from his university office without even a handshake to say goodbye, armed gangs were spreading fear all over Croatia and Bosnia. By the summer of 1999, when that Balkan Macbeth Slobodan Milošević, scenting defeat and full of bloodlust, decided to clear out Kosovo as though it were a gym that needed repainting, and to murder, burn or blow up anybody who got in his way, my father began to list to the left. He kept bumping into the furniture and one day he followed my mother to the bank veering from one parked car to another. He was determined that he, gallant knight that he was, must save my mother from the bandits of the market economy whose latest trick was to rob and kill old people tottering to collect their pensions.

The last passionate political arguments in the hall of the flat in Németvölgyi Road took place in the early spring of 1992, when my father tried to convince me that Milošević, the last bastion of the principle of socialist collective ownership, was facing an Islamic fundamentalist in the Bosnian leader Alija Izetbegović. While occasionally admitting his historical achievements, my father could never forgive Comrade Tito for becoming a running dog of imperialism and allowing the system that millions (including himself) had staked their lives on to collapse from within. In 1989, when Party official Milošević came to power in the by-then somewhat looser Yugoslavian Federation, my father recovered the hope that this hard-boiled apparatchik would save the sinking ship of socialism. It had been years since we had conducted any kind of political conversation but this storm of terrible events in a neighbouring country wrought such elemental passions in both of us that we were screaming at each other, red-faced, between the crowded bookshelves of the hall, just like in the good old days.

'Mass murderer! Manipulator! I don't care what Izetbegović wrote fifteen years ago! What do you mean socialism? What do you mean fundamentalism? Excuses!!! He is a power-obsessed psychopath!' I was yelling, quite beside myself.

Poor Hegel, Gegel and Bebel were in a tizzy. They didn't know whether to laugh or be seriously scared. They had forgotten that we used to have such screaming matches regularly. When we had done with the steam and smoke we went unwillingly to put on our jackets because my mother chased us out of the flat and told us to go for a good walk. Mother was, of course, right as usual. By the time we reached the corner of Pagony Street we had calmed down.

'Lucky that Danilo Kiš did not live to see this,' I said by way of reconciliation.

My father hummed in agreement. Not that he was exactly a fan of Kiš, but I did once shove a short story by Kiš under his nose, the one involving the murder of Rosa

Luxemburg. He had hummed in exactly the same way then. I left the book for him in the hope that he would read the rest. When I asked for it back some weeks later, it turned out that it had vanished into the vortex of his study and I was obliged to buy a new copy.

In the early autumn of 1993 I received a call from an acquaintance to say that Zdravko was in Geneva and, if I had time, I should join them both for dinner. Zdravko taught history at the university in Sarajevo and had been allowed out of the besieged city to take part in an international conference. Two years before, when we met at a similar conference in Prague, he had been a handsome young man who spoke enthusiastically about the possibility of a global civil society. This time a grey-haired old man with burned-out eyes faced me across the table. He had the same grey look as all those other men I had seen in documentary films about Bosnia. It was as if, irrespective of their ages, the brutal annihilation of their land had hung the sign of death over them. Zdravko didn't say much, and said practically nothing about the city.

Screwing the thin white napkins into paper balls, I leaned against the cool tiles that covered the wall of the kebab restaurant where we were eating and listened to the conversation without saying anything myself. I was ashamed to be living in this calm and comfortable city, just two hours away from the massacre that was dealing a last blow to Europe, while also despairing about my father. Of course, my heart was heavy on account of Bosnia as well, but now, suddenly face to face with this prematurely aged young man, I thought it was wrong to feel such despair at my father's single, not untimely, approaching natural death. The devastation leisurely working its way through my father's cells was, after all, a natural and dignified form of last rite, something a man can feel a part of. Suddenly the whole thing seemed dwarfed by the devastation wrought beyond my country's southern borders. My father's approaching one-off death had cast a shadow over my life as though it were something unique, threatening the natural order of the world. Our neighbours' reality involved the possibility of death at any moment, a possibility that people had had to learn to live with, much as they had learned to live with low water pressure or constantly late buses. Meaningless mass destruction was a legitimate part of our apparently orderly lives, something we could indeed live with. The fact that we could do so quite calmly raised doubts about the credibility of either reality.

Right in the middle of the Bosnian war, for some mysterious reason that I can't recall, I landed at the old airfield of Budapest. I sat down on the steps to the arrivals hall and waited for whoever was coming to fetch me. In the empty airport car park stood an enormous, sparkling clean bus with the word Yugoslavia proudly displayed on its side. It was a warm, late autumn day and the sun was blinding but its rays no longer warmed me. I sat in the deserted square and felt an odd calm. It was as if time had stopped and I felt the kind of unexpected happiness that I had felt in my innocent youth. Perhaps it was all a bad dream? Perhaps Yugoslavia was not falling to pieces? Perhaps the dead weren't really dead? Perhaps my father was in good health? Perhaps it was possible to get back to a point where everything was all right?

'Seriously, darling, how far back do you want to go?' murmured the voice of the socialist realist co-tenant in my head.

But I paid no attention. I was sunning myself on the sparkling wings of illusion.

ଓ

One day when I arrived relatively early at the hospital I sat on my father's bed and watched him washing. He washed slowly and systematically. Face, neck, ears, the shaving foam behind his ears, under the arms, his chest and the upper part of his back. The careful movements that covered every part of the skin were a reminder of his childhood, when there was no properly equipped bathroom and he had to bend over a full basin or a tub to perform the most thorough of ablutions, and though the luxury of running water might have rendered the whole process unnecessary, the habit persisted even in this last phase of his life when my father had to lean against the basin because he was no longer capable of standing on his feet. Our habits of movement never leave us, remaining with us to the end so that we should be able to hang on to something firm when everything around us is gradually sinking; our fixed gestures, our turns of phrase, the shreds and patches of our thoughts all trying to render familiar our temporary lodging, to stuff the gaping holes in the fabric of our existence through which howls the cold wind of non-being. It's quite pointless for him to wash so thoroughly, I thought, because my mother will soon be here and she'll help him out to the neglected shower from which unknown hands have long stolen both the handle and the shower-head, and she will carefully sit him down on the one remaining plastic chair and scrub him down like a helpless overgrown baby.

Perhaps this is what old age is, I thought distractedly as I watched the fugitive drops of water run down his back, reaching the shore of his crumpled striped pyjamas, while the outside world finds ever-narrower channels by which to enter the consciousness, its place being gradually usurped by habit. One becomes a kind of self-powered automaton that conscientiously grinds through its established routine, now and then dropping the odd hollow phrase that has ever less to do with the constantly changing world beyond; a desolate machine whose battery is running out, that stops in the middle of a room or on a street corner and the world pays no attention at all, but rushes by on its business, until tender hands finally pick it up and clear it out of the way. That might be what old age is, and my dying father – who has never wanted to be old – might have to take a quick course on the difficult subject of ageing now. As I watched his slow, methodical movements, a poem by the Transylvanian poet Árpád Farkas came to my mind, 'When Old Men Wash' – the one in which he talks about old people bending over a sink, trying to wash themselves clean of all the filth of the twentieth century. Are we the last generation for whom poetry remains a natural language, for whom verses spring readily to mind and are constantly on the tips of our tongues whenever we fall in love, or break up, or suffer, or go mad? Who nowadays has the time to contemplate a line of poetry?

Farkas's poem reminded me of an evening long ago when my father came home unexpectedly early and found my sister and me still awake though in our pyjamas. He didn't even bother to take off his jacket, but washed his hands and came straight into our bedroom to say goodnight. We were bouncing wildly on our beds and were choking with laughter, yelling: 'This Ady poem is mad. Ady is an idiot. Just look at this rubbish! "Those without wine had better run,/This is the black piano, son!"'

My father leant against the doorframe and gazed at our hysterics in astonishment. For a while he simply stood there quietly smiling, as he did when he wanted to find a clinching argument, then he left the room and returned with a small black leather-bound volume.

'Listen to this!' he said and he read the whole of 'The Earl's Threshing-floor'. 'The Black Piano' was one of Ady's first Symbolist poems, while 'The Earl's Threshing-floor' was a dramatic description of the misery of the rural poor in early twentieth-century Hungary.

When my father finished there was an awed silence. I had an enormous lump in my throat and, if I weren't so ashamed, I would have burst into tears. My father smiled.

'Is this mad, too?' he asked.

We sat on our beds, stunned. My father didn't even wait for an answer, but wished us goodnight and switched off the light. That night we didn't keep getting up, but went obediently to sleep without a word. We didn't even have our usual bedtime chatter.

'Do you remember "The Earl's Threshing-floor"?' I asked my father when, having finished towelling himself down, he proceeded slowly to button up his pyjama top. He smiled but I couldn't work out if it was because he remembered the incident or if, in his own clumsy way, he wanted to do no more than indicate that he was happy that I was here, that he had succeeded in washing, in scrambling into his pyjama top and that now, having done with all this hard work, he could rest satisfied. I didn't pursue the matter. I didn't particularly want to question him about the past; I did not want him to think I was thinking he was dying.

This story tells you everything about my father as regards the craft of parenting. He never taught me to write, to read, to swim, or to cycle; never took me to the playground; never came to parents' meetings; never put a plaster on my cuts and bruises; never read me goodnight stories; in other words, he never lived up to the image of the father I expected for my children. But when he did rarely appear, he always gave me something to help me along. Once he consoled me when I was unhappily in love, with all the concomitant despair and fire of first love; on another occasion he explained why it was always necessary to be honest; on yet another he told me that I must be responsible for my actions. Everything else I learned from others. It was a little, short-haired communist veteran who taught me to swim, for example. Her skin was as brown and wrinkled as one of those calfskin handbags so fashionable at the time. I've no idea how or why, but this old lady took me under her wing at the Római part baths where the big shots of the Party would go to swim;

she taught me how to breathe regularly, how to swim with my head under water, how to turn, how to dive, and how, at the end, to take first a scalding, then an icy shower. I never learned the lady's name and nobody in the family remembers her, but whenever and wherever I find myself in any kind of water, when I turn on to my back, let my head float and begin to paddle in the waves with my palms half-closed, I thank her for the lessons.

While on the subject of swimming lessons, I should mention the crowded beach of some union resort by Lake Balaton where my father suspended me in the water by the straps of my swimming costume. I shook in terror as he assured me that I wouldn't sink, although I swallowed more water than I trod. Years later, when I visited my parents on another holiday, I watched my father swimming. His head was lifted painfully clear of the water so he shouldn't get water on the thick lenses of his glasses and so ruin his clear view. Even there, in the very centre of the broad lake, he had to be on constant alert: the glasses mustn't ever be removed. Fully submerging himself in the water was as dangerous as diving into life; there were too many risks attached.

☙

The summer my father died, when once again I set about a course of daily visits to the hospital, I relived the months of seven years before when the sequence of recovery, relapse and complications following the first operation sent us scuttling all over town through a series of similar run-down hospitals. I saw again those long corridors, the uncomfortable benches of which there were never enough, and the patients, their legs swollen with standing about, their mouths dry with fear, clutching their medical notes, while ambulances howled and builders drilled around them because in hospitals there is always something to repair. In the minds of the fearful the beating of hammers tends to conjure the nailing down of a coffin lid, though, and I saw again how anxiously the patients noted the enormous eyes of those rolling off the ambulances, the pale luminous faces of the newly afflicted visible above the trolley blankets, or watched the lime-white faces of other people being wheeled out of the operating theatre, people with eyes that were expressionless, and might remain expressionless for ever. I saw the sick, surrounded by anxious relatives, who expected the Messiah himself to enter every time the door opened, a Messiah who would save them from the wicked disease that had treacherously infiltrated their minds and bodies. But when the white uniforms and gentle shuffle of Scholl sandals vanished behind mysterious glass doors, they lost hope and would sink into themselves again, their flushed cheeks fading, so that a couple of hours later they were no longer animated because now they understood that they too were assigned to taking their place in the constantly turning machinery, lethargically accepting the results of their examination, the date set for the operation and the details of post-operation procedure as if it had nothing to do with them. They would not protest when the knives came out because they had neither the strength nor the desire to do so; they had become indifferent, their hearts numbed, having realised that they were no longer human beings but merely cases in a hospital; just the matter of one ward or another, a file that enters the registry and proceeds from there, in perfectly ruly fashion, to the dustbin. It was a great distinction for my father in the hospital, that busy antechamber of death, that while remaining as nameless and impersonal as the rest, he could still be addressed as 'the Professor'.

Fifth

Time slowed down the summer my father died. Every day there was some important event that stood out, distinguishing itself from the great confluence of currents that is time: one day he felt a little better, another he could walk right down the corridor, on a third he was no longer able to button his pyjama top. The days before the operation were particularly crowded and hectic, and if I stood still for a moment I immediately felt dizzy: it was like falling slowly but unstoppably down a bottomless pit. Everyone went about their necessary business, following the rhythms of the hospital. There was the shopping, the arrangements, the doctors, the nurses, the entertaining of the children, the consoling of my mother, all the various toings and froings. We concentrated on our tasks: it was as if the thought of the most natural and most dreadful end of life had never occurred to us and we were simply floating towards it; as if we didn't know my father was about to cross the threshold into the void. Death was not in the picture yet, it was biding its time and, though it cast a shadow over everything, we told each other it was merely a passing cloud. That was right until we were told he was dead, when everything in the picture became the domain of death. One day I was surprised to notice a black vest in my shopping basket.

'I don't know what to prepare for, a long-drawn-out period of dying or a funeral,' I told my friend Justine as we pushed our daughters on the playground swings the day before I left Geneva. I could talk like this while I was far away. But from the moment the plane touched down at Ferihegy airport the possibility of my father dying never once entered the conversation.

We had lived in Geneva seven years by then. When, after years of itinerant living, I had settled there, my father remarked: 'At least it's a safe place.' Some part of him might perhaps have added: 'And at least you avoid the expense of escaping.'

My father's second remark was that, if champions of freedom such as Jean-Jacques Rousseau and Lenin could leave their marks on the town, there couldn't be much wrong with it. My mother didn't like Geneva. For her, the decisive factor was the memory of visiting this Swiss paradise on their first trip to the West in the mid-1970s. They travelled with their scraped-together dollars, staying at cheap, dirty hotels, or with the network of comrades the Party had stationed abroad: they were real explorers. My father acted as guide and my mother was happy to rely on him. Then they arrived at this crisply laundered town where houses, streets and faces – indeed everything – is unnaturally smooth. One day in the supermarket my mother knocked over a bottle of olive oil. The uniformed and suited shop assistants looked on scandalised while the pool of oil spread, as oil tends to, slowly, unhurriedly between the shards of broken glass. My mother apologised profusely to everyone in her incomprehensible native language, and searched feverishly in the plastic bag she took with her everywhere for a packet of paper hankies with which to wipe away the evidence of her crime. No one raised a finger to help, no one tried to stop her; they all gazed on, calm and patient, as she blotted the pool at her feet and finally threw the oily paper handkerchief into the bin that of course she only located after looking around for a while.

This incident, which my mother would often recount full of indignation as if she had never got over it, reminded me, unwillingly, of that photograph taken at the time of the *Anschluss* in which the elderly Jew with the long beard is shown scrubbing a Vienna street with a toothbrush while German soldiers stand around laughing, their boots polished to a high gloss. It's true that my mother was surrounded only by lacquered shoes, not boots, and that she was not about to be shot through the head, but based on this image I had formed an opinion of Geneva long before I set foot there. When life eventually took me to Geneva and it turned out that I would spend a considerable amount of time there, I cheered myself with the thought that the great genius Jorge Luis Borges wanted to die there. Typical of Borges, of course, he would fill my head with all sorts of contradictory things but I couldn't decide what his true message was. I had been living in Geneva ten years before

I discovered Borges' obscure grave in the city and what was written on it. It was a sentence from the forgotten tenth-century English poem 'The Battle of Maldon': 'And ne forhtedon na', 'And be not afraid'.

Despite having drunk the bitter-sweet brew of exile for a dozen years now, I still can't work out whether that blank Genevan look covered a real emptiness or a well-concealed sorrow. That is despite having read the obligatory books as well as Elias Canetti's Swiss memoirs and suggested reading list about the country. After some years of strenuous effort I decided that, while I would never feel at home here, at least people would leave me in peace. Politics can be repellent even in seasoned democracies like Switzerland, but here it doesn't poison everyday life, at least not to the level it does in Hungary. France Culture and the BBC were always worth listening to, irrespective of which governments were in power. That teachers teach their classes, that doctors tend to their patients, that policemen support the law, that locksmiths repair locks and that 'small fish coyly spawn', as Miklós Radnóti puts it, goes without saying, whatever the government. It's not quite so simple at home.

The heaviest burden laid on us by our fathers who were busy building really-existing socialism was the assumption that individual life was of no value. The Horthy régime had not rated individual life particularly highly, and the new ideology had turned life upside down precisely so that human dignity should be restored. 'Nothing that is human is alien to me,' wrote the Roman playwright Terence: those words were inscribed on the walls of our classrooms (as a quote from Marx), precisely when everything human was being swept away. In the beginning it might have been an understandable sacrifice on the sacred altar of progress or one of the necessary casualties along the pilgrimage route, but step by step it became an essential characteristic of the system. The Gulag was the physical embodiment of a philosophy in which human life counted for nothing. And little Gulags were created in the schools and hospitals, on the tram and in the press, screaming at you: 'You are nothing! You are nothing!' And however loudly the commercial placards bellowed their messages from the crumbling façades of our buildings, however free we were to choose between twenty-five varieties of yoghurt, and despite being able to found parties, start up newspapers or establish institutions, we were unable to cast off this most heavy of burdens. It was there in those who barged past others in the queue at the post office, in the way people cursed each other on the bus, in schools where children were abused and where abuse was silently tolerated, in official corridors where people were made to wait for hours, in unanswered letters and unreturned phone calls, in everyday minor compromises, in our guts, even in our dreams, and it was impossible to know when it might finally vanish.

My father found the country he was trying to save just as much 'a dreadful hole' as his distant soul buddy the great orientalist Ignác Goldziher did, but, like the Professor, he never thought to leave it. His sense of mission tied him to the soil, and that loyalty to the soil was bound together with his almost mystical faith in his mission, inherited from Jewish messianism, which helped him overcome various failures and humiliations. Maybe he himself did not notice how well he mixed his antecedents' romantic patriotism with the proletarian internationalism preached by the Party. Whenever we went on a field trip with my mothers' students, my father was as happy to sing the Polish revolutionary anthem the '*Warszawianka*' as he was the old Hungarian folk song that goes: 'I'm leaving, I'm leaving / I'm taking the long road / From the dust of that long road / I'll weave myself a coat.' Despite all this, he was far less upset than my mother when I took up residence abroad. He had long given up the hope that I might be a comrade in the struggle for the Cause. I had no longer a mission at home, so, fortunately, I could not be regarded as a traitor, but instead could function as a sort of foreign correspondent enjoying special observer privileges. Whenever I visited home, he politely admired the gifts of Swiss chocolate and the Bowmore whisky intended to compensate for the lack of Ararat cognac, but what he really wanted were my impressions of life abroad, and he continued to enquire about these until illness forced him to retreat into himself.

I myself naturally continue to regard Budapest as my home, not Geneva, where I live. After all, how can anyone feel at home in a city where they leave the lights on in the corridors? I once even asked the electrician why, if you please, are the lights left on all night in the stairwell? Of course I didn't mention Pilinszky's '*Quatran*' that came to my mind whenever I saw the illuminated long corridors late at night:

Nails asleep under frozen sand.
Nights soaked in poster-loneliness.
You left the light on in the corridor.
Today my blood is shed.

But, however he tried, he couldn't convince me that it was cheaper to leavc them on than to install an automatic system.

In Geneva everything is solemn, spare and regulated, even humour has certain limits. One misses the blurring of lines, those secret nooks. No romantic feeling for strollers through the Old Town, not the kind you get in the Castle district in Buda, in Hradčany Castle in Prague; or the warm orange-brown coloured streets of Bologna, where the sheer material of the city plays on the senses and where getting to the marble white central square is an offence to modesty; or in Barcelona, where, even putting the work of Gaudí aside, you are continually tempted to run your hand along any surface whatsoever, including the pavements. Even the café door-handles are so nice to touch that they are hard to let go. I won't keep on about Budapest, where the Danube flows so regally through the swelling hills and buildings, and – that's quite enough of that!

(That is your socialist realist fellow lodger speaking, who can't bear talk like this.)

So where was I?

Ever since the glorious triumph of the Reformation the heavens have been like a brow frowning over Calvin's city. People look grimly disciplined and get on with their work.

There is just one majestic and ungovernably free inhabitant of the city: the lake. Without the lake I couldn't bear to live here, not for a moment. No doubt it's no accident that the heraldic emblem of the city, the 130-metre-high fountain, one enormous phallic symbol, is situated dead centre of the lake and that tourists from all over the world, of either gender, all fully equipped with cameras and videos, love to have their picture taken against it. Snap, snap. Zzzrrrr. The lake tends mostly to belong to our part of the city, a quarter of ill-repute full of immigrants and simple natives, situated in the elongated triangle formed by the main railway terminal, the red-light district and the big hotels. Every morning after I have taken the children to school, my first steps lead me here. It's not a proper day if it does not begin here.

I leave behind the lakeshore's heavy, charmless civic buildings that act as bulwarks against the burgeoning chaos behind them. I turn my back on banks that look like churches, on the hurrying feet of the faithful servants of Mammon, on gentlemen with ties and briefcases and pink newspapers under their arms, on young women wearing identical smiles and earphones tucked into their ears as they make their way from car to entrance so that nothing of the world's noise should accidentally reach them. I turn my back on the hotels with their glazed fronts where bored couples sink into deep leather chairs and where early morning business meetings proceed with the stirring of coffee cups. I pass the Palais Wilson, which is the only lakeshore building to remain solemn and harmonious – maybe because it recalls the time when the League of Nations gathered here to debate and repair what remained of the world after the First World War.

Once the Palais Wilson vanishes behind me, I enter another dimension. The space opens up. The eye caresses the sky, the water and the distant blue mountains, the trees, the harbour, the scattered buildings in the park, with nothing to detain it, even for a moment. Here nature infiltrates the domain of this severe, self-denying town like the advance guard of the great dark wood, however the town tries to encircle and control it. Here one notices how a single cone suddenly opens up and disperses the seeds, that the pine on top of the hill has lurched into a dance in the tentative sunlight, and that barely a hundred metres away, despite the grumbling car noise in the background, one can hear the heavy beat of swans' wings as they rise from the water. Eventually I have to return to the high enclosing walls, but my heart, my eye and my lungs remember the wings.

Had the Great Planner ever got round to consulting me, I would have chosen a city better fitted to my affinities, but He never did. On the question of freedom of choice, a subject we might ponder while we're at it, it occurs to me that we are a privileged generation to have grown up with a sense of long-term security. We could still believe that, with a little help, we were able to predict the world, and that given, let's say, twenty-five years, we might prepare ourselves for it. But today I can only spread my hands and admit I haven't a clue what's to come, never mind what I would like to happen. But it surprises even me that, after moving around for several years, I should have wound up in an immaculate town like Geneva, on the ever faster hamster-wheel of everyday life, work and child care, in a world of dirty realism, not of curing people or even sick societies, but producing specialist papers on how they might be cured.

I moved to Geneva to join the man who was to become my husband, Steven. Like my friend Elie, whom I met in the early 1980s in Budapest, Steven was an American Jew and, before we met, he too had been travelling around Eastern Europe looking for the sparks of freedom. But, unlike Elie, he wasn't in love with it: he was trying to understand it. Elie was spellbound by the intimate smell of humanity, the discreet charm of absurdity and destruction that hung about our picturesque domain in those times; Steven hated to see all that ground under the heels of the police. His indignation prevented him from succumbing to such discreet charm and continually spurred him to seek out the possibilities for change. He happened to be concentrating on the Germans, who were divided by a wall and by two supposedly different ways of thinking, when the phone rang and he was called to Prague. This was in the euphoric months following the collapse of the Iron Curtain in 1989, when it seemed that we were entering an age of genuine choice among possible futures; that once we had succeeded in freeing ourselves from the false prophets of salvation, we need not immediately follow robber barons for whom freedom, equality and brotherhood, or even honest business or the concept of long-term rationality, were the relics of a vanished age that could be consigned to the wastebasket. One evening Steven appeared at an international conference of those who were dreaming of a new Europe among the sumptuous walls of the art nouveau Obecní Dům, the Municipal House, where my long-dead grandparents used to go to concerts, and asked me if I fancied a stroll. We set off down narrow cobbled streets, watched the black swans on the Vltava and talked as if we had known each other for ever.

Apart from my father, Steven is the only man who can really make me lose my temper. I have known others who have made me despair, but he and my father were the only men I could scream at, red in the face. Steven didn't like my father. In the seven years of suspense between my father's two bouts of illness, true to his character, he offered his continual rational support, rational not only because he finds high-emotion scenes difficult, but because to him, as no doubt to the rest of the world, my father was just an old Stalinist who had been sitting on the bench of the accused, a seat he had earned time and again with every dramatic turn in our region's history. Steven had grown up on the writings of Victor Serge, Edward Thompson and Hal Draper; he understood very well the significance of the workers' councils of 1956 and Solidarność, and had read Trotsky when I was still gazing at the empty space Trotsky had left behind on the photo of Comrade Lenin addressing the masses. For him, those communists who forgot the dreams of a free and just society and once they had come to power just hung on to it for decades, whatever the cost, were unforgivable criminals. Thanks to the gun-toting, baying Cossacks, half of Steven's ancestors had been eradicated and the other half had been exiled from their never-to-be-forgotten Odessa, so he had grown up in idyllic California, where he hadn't had much chance to meet too many living examples of Eastern European adherents of really-existing Stalinism. I suspect my father occupied all the seats on the bench of the accused in his mind. There they were in a row, closely pressed against each other, all those Fülöp Hollós, listening, stubbornly and uncomprehendingly, occasionally indignantly, to the never-ending charges against them. And more than likely they were wondering how they might turn the whole thing into a trial like that of the Bulgarian communist Georgi Dimitrov, in which the accused turned the table on his prosecutors.

Luckily, my father was not apprised of the storms he had caused in my husband's soul. They rarely met in person, and language set a benign limit on their foggy communication. I alone knew of the insoluble, fierce antagonism between these two decisive figures in my life, but naturally I kept deadly silent about it. We had some mighty quarrels on this account at the safe distance of our Geneva flat. Not that I didn't admit Steven was right, but I wasn't willing to drop my father in the dustbin of history, not with my own hands. His views, his work in the Party, the Party itself, yes – but he himself, no.

America, America. The first time I visited the United States, years before I met Steven, like many others, I was impressed by the freedom, the apparently endless possibilities, the dazzling wealth of people, cultures, styles, the myth on which America is built. I was living in neighbouring Mexico at the time and the only reason that I crossed the border was that I badly wanted to see my old friend Miki Winter, who had become a professor at a leading American university, and Elie, who was visiting home. At the same time I could put my head in the lion's mouth and take a look around, a prospect that excited my curiosity. I had to answer a vast number of questions for the entry visa: to what race did I belong and what political party was I a member of, among other things. There was a long, anxious queue at passports, periodically examined by police dogs on leashes. This felt like home. When I finally managed to enter the stronghold of imperialism, a wild cheerfulness seized me. Right in the middle of New York, among the endless queues of cars, the skyscrapers and flashing neon signs, between a Sikh in a turban and an enormous black guy, a kaftan-wearing orthodox Jew was shouting down a wall-mounted public telephone in a thick Szabolcs-Szatmár accent.

'It's me! Where am I? Am I awake?' I too found myself shouting down the telephone.

'Where are you? Can't you just tell me where you are?' Elie bellowed back a little impatiently.

I had to put the phone down to read the sign on the street corner.

My friend Elie was a New York Jewish boy, from the third generation of an immigrant Russian family who had long forgotten the language, their grandfather's original name and the stories passed down from father to son, because the struggle for existence that consumed every last bit of energy had completely drained even the possibility of nostalgia from their minds. Like my future husband, Elie carried the holy trinity of persecution, flight and survival in his cells, but, unlike my future husband, he felt it was important to give these feelings names. When, at the beginning of the 1980s, at roughly the age of thirty, he visited Eastern Europe for the first time and saw the russet brown fences made of wide wooden boards that looked exactly like his grandfather's in Queens that at that time still counted as a village, he felt he had arrived home. The first person who had taught me that being a Jew was not an agonising secret, something to be ashamed of, but a fact that might occasionally be a source of strength, had been Vera, my childhood physics and chemistry teacher at the elementary school in Németvölgyi Road. Elie was the second.

Elie had often visited me in Budapest and now it was his turn to show me proudly around New York. New York had everything and every kind of person. People were ready to get into conversation, just like at home; this was the empire of immigrants where no one had the privilege of the first-born, or, to put it more precisely, those who might have had such a call had long been wiped out in the name of God and freedom. The bookshops, the museums, the skyscrapers and zigzagging fire-escapes, the walk down Brighton Beach, the alleys of the Lower East Side, the Brooklyn Botanic Garden, the Thai soups and Russian bortsch: the town received us like a vast big-hearted playground. We played hide-and-seek between the supporting columns of the World Trade Center and, ugh, how ugly, we cried. We only liked the old skyscrapers, the ones on which Mexican migrant workers had laboured, those whose bodies still guarded the faint memory of the road to the Sun God and who weren't scared of the dizzying heights when they were building these big money palaces for the white men.

One Sunday morning, Elie took me to a klezmer concert, where a childhood playmate of his, Andy Statman, was playing. I had never heard of klezmer, the celebratory music of the Ashkenazic Jews, but through the long subway ride Elie briefed me and entertained me with stories of the adventures of the rock band he and Andy had founded when they were adolescents. Before they went on stage, we met Andy's klezmorim in the corridor: three Americans, a Yemeni, two Iraqis, an Ethiopian and two Russians. A vast crowd had gathered in the auditorium while we were talking. As we entered the loud, packed hall, the thought struck me that it was the first time in my life that I had been with so many Jews at once. Back home, in the Nagyfuvaros Street synagogue that I had started to attend after Vera died, there were only a handful of people in the gallery, even on Yom Kippur, and on the rare occasion that there was a Jewish theme at the clandestine 'flying university', there were never more than fifteen people present.

Along the rows of seats my fellow Jews started by loudly quarrelling over something, then calming down, then pretty soon putting their arms around each other before starting to dance. Up on stage the one-time rocker was warming to his task with ever more enthusiasm. The tunes shifted into ever more ecstatic sound. It was as if every single shriek of the high-pitched clarinet were peeling away a protective layer of my soul. Very soon my whole being had set out on a passionate and unpredictable journey. Everything was opening up. Beyond the topmost branches of the trees stretched an endless sky to which my soul completely abandoned itself. Then, suddenly, I fell into the deepest pit. It was dark and cold, and I was hemmed in by thick damp walls. A little way off I seemed to see a faint flickering light. I tried to turn towards it, but my body felt leaden, and invisible weights obstructed me. I could hardly breathe. The smell of vomit and excreta mingled with the all-pervasive smell of death. Straining every muscle, I tried to make my way to the door when I saw a pile of corpses on the benches beside me, the bodies there hadn't been time to carry out into the frozen yard of the synagogue. There was a figure leaning over the Ark of the Covenant. I don't know whether I cried out or simply whimpered, but Elie and another strong lad helped me out of the hall into the fresh air and trees full of birds.

'Don't move, I'll get you some water,' said Elie, and propped me up against the wall.

'The trees are twittering,' I mumbled to myself while slowly sliding to the ground. Elie handed me a glass of water, his hands shaking.

'Are you pregnant or something?' he asked anxiously. There were tiny beads of sweat above his lips.

'Am I pregnant?' I asked in terror.

'I'm pregnant with the past,' I said as he packed me into a taxi.

'You're delirious,' he answered nervously, then turned to the driver to tell him where to go.

I was shivering as with a fever. We went home and I used what remained of my strength to drag myself into bed and pulled the covers over me. Elie was in the kitchen clattering about with the kettle. I heard his footsteps as he came in with the steaming tea, then I fell into a deep and dreamless sleep.

A good fifteen years later I visited Elie in Berlin, where he had settled, to my great surprise, after wandering around all over Europe. We were sitting in the yard next to the Garden of Exile and Emigration beside the Jewish Museum. The imposing building was still resoundingly empty. We walked round it in silence and agreed that it should remain empty. Out in the garden Elie talked of the poems of Rose Ausländer, I of the documentary films of the Cambodian Rithy Panh. We weren't the first, I told him, and we wouldn't be the last. Behind our fathers' bodies, haphazardly piled and thrown into ditches or burned to ashes, there were long queues of dismembered Armenians, Indonesians killed by machine-gun fire from helicopters, Cambodians with slit throats, Tutsis hacked to pieces with machetes, Bosnians burned to death in their own stables, and all those I have forgotten, an endless abhorrent stream of them. We sat in the garden where the first buds of spring had already opened, listening to the birds' chorus, and I wondered about what kind of gardens our children would find themselves sitting in.

☙

So, long before Elie, the first person who had talked to me about Jews had been Vera, my elementary school teacher. Vera was a brilliant teacher and an irresistibly charismatic person. I had been so eager to please her that I had learnt by heart Mendeleev's Periodic Table, the three states of water, and my first poems by Attila József. She taught science, but she knew more poems by heart than any literature teacher in school. This surprised me at first, but she just laughed and asked: 'Why so surprised, my innocent bumpkin, don't you know we're run by a bunch of good-for-nothings?'

I had been enchanted by her since our first physics lesson. My father had arrived from Moscow the night before. All his returns were ceremonial occasions, but this time he had bought me an unusual present: an enormous school satchel with several pockets. When I dragged my lovely burden to school the next morning, arriving in class a good ten minutes late, the new teacher didn't reach for the register to note my lateness but gave me a brilliant smile and remarked: 'I see you are set for a long voyage with that sea chest of yours. I hope you will have the stamina to fill it.'

In the winter of 1944 Vera was watching from a neighbour's doorway as Arrow Cross youths marched her father from the flat where the family had successfully hidden out, until someone gave him away in a flush of patriotism. A child she knew pulled her and her mother into the doorway and later showed her around the house, in whose cellar they could take refuge with their forged papers, because the air-raid warden was a decent man. Vera's father was murdered at Buchenwald and she herself would have died of pneumonia in the damp cellar had she not been saved by a young man who had escaped the work camps, returned to Budapest and, disguised as an Arrow Cross officer, set to save his fellow Jews condemned to death. After the war, this brave young man was beaten for months in the cellars of AVO, the Hungarian KGB, because of his stolen Arrow Cross uniform; another keen patriot reported him for collaboration. The AVO officers would have overlooked the collaboration but, since the young man refused to work for the newly founded Ministry of the Interior, they sentenced him to death. We couldn't claim that the same ardent patriot reported Vera's father and her saviour, but my beloved capital has never been short of ardent patriots ready to report on their fellow citizens. Pneumonia had another go at removing Vera from the planet at the end of the 1950s, when she and her young son were holed up in a tiny flat with no amenities because her husband had been jailed for his activities in the 1956 uprising. By a miracle it was the same disguised young man who hurried to help her again. Having escaped execution and having learned that no one from his family had survived the deportations, he had succeeded in getting himself smuggled over the border by hiding in a coffin. Once over, he didn't stop till he got to America, where he became Mr Lang, a successful restaurant owner. When Mr Lang discovered that Vera was in trouble again, he sent her valuable albums of artists' prints – real rarities in those days in a Hungary plagued by every other kind of shortage. Vera never even opened the plastic packing, but hurried down to the Central Antiquarium and sold the books so she and her son could eat for a fortnight. Years later I would console myself with the thought that I might have seen some of those very same albums in the reading rooms of the Ernő Szabó central library.

It wasn't pneumonia that did for Vera in the end, but the white tablets she filled her hands with and forced down her throat in a room she rented for the day via the national holiday booking office. It was the mid-1980s and one could sense the world preparing itself for dramatic change: its joints were creaking dangerously. Strange articles began to appear in the press, people were talking more freely, there were arguments instead of statements. Vera's son had grown up and her husband had fallen in love with a twenty-year-old woman. Her infallible instincts told Vera it was the beginning of a new stage in her life, but it wasn't one she cared to enter. She had had enough of survival. It was no use being appointed at last to a position more fitting to her talents; it was no use being surrounded by friends and admirers; the struggle had worn her out. Maybe she felt that death, her most faithful suitor, who had been wooing her her entire life, finally deserved to be granted his wish. She rented the tourist office room so that no one should surprise her and quietly moved into the world of shadows.

ᴓ

It was a strange experience living in Geneva through the seven years between my father's two bouts of illness. Constantly moving between places changed my sense of time: the unremitting flow was broken. Being now here, now there, became a formative experience that intensified not only the experience of all that happened, but also my sense of distance from events. The parallel realities I regularly moved between as on a paternoster taught me the relative value of things. It wasn't just that the reality of my father's approaching death grew ever clearer, but so did the realisation that I myself was not vital to the working of things in either place.

Each time I returned to Geneva I tried to live as though

life was normal and forget the sword of Damocles poised above our heads. But the days were soaked through with tension that distance only increased. Every time the phone rang I leapt to pick it up; every time I said goodbye to my father my stomach shrank with worry. And since it was impossible to resolve the anxieties by pottering about with small distractions – I couldn't help him on with his coat, I couldn't prop him up on his way to the bathroom, I couldn't stand in a queue for his prescriptions at the stale-smelling chemist's – helplessness vastly increased the anxiety. It was a genie escaped from the bottle, towering above my head, a constant threat. I'd get a panic attack at the most surprising moments, feeling I had failed to do something that could have changed the course of events, that my father's life, my own life, was inevitably slipping through my fingers. As soon as we touched down at Ferihegy Terminal 2, the anxiety immediately left me. I was suddenly calm, almost cheerful, because the problem, with all its dramatic and comical moments, was soluble and at hand. I could do something about it: it was no longer a threatening genie that only made me tremble.

Since my father died, we take the train home. There's nothing particularly urgent to attend to, nothing to force us to save hours: we can give the journey the attention it deserves. On the way back, en route to Geneva, after the change of trains at dawn, my eyes slowly adjust to a different set of realities. The enormous sky with its drifting, pink-edged clouds hovering over meadows sweating in the summer heat gives way to the calm green of forests, cool mountains and scarlet geraniums budding on windowsills. There are no coils of cable lying about in the stations, no carriages with broken windows and graffiti. Neat villages ache with centuries of reassuring order, fortresses rise from hilltops, every stone in place. Before setting off, I stuff the two enormous black holdalls not just with clothes and my mother's miraculous home-made jam, but with unread newspapers and books, books, books, from Zsigmond Móricz through to Péter Nádas. And this is what I drag along with me, puffing and panting, moaning and despairing, from the Keleti, the Eastern Terminal in Budapest, all the way to Cornavin in Geneva, in the hope that these smuggled items might illuminate my life far away from home. But then a thousand everyday tasks propel me unnoticed between the local parameters and I find myself doing no more than looking longingly at the books and the unread piles of *Libération* and the *New York Review of Books* as they settle on the piles of *Élet és Irodalom*, the Hungarian literary weekly, and *Magyar Narancs*, a critical magazine, great piles of which surround my desk, agitating for attention for a while but eventually giving up and slowly turning yellow. Whenever Steven wants to tidy up, I scream at him and chase him out of the study, just as my father did with my mother: once there is no more room on the floor, I shovel everything in the cupboard until, having handed in a work that has passed several deadlines, and completely exhausted, I make a mighty effort to catch up with time, trying to become a contemporary of our age.

Author remarks: As far as catching up with time goes, hardly any success has been registered.
This is how I move between the two cities, several times a year, as though I have forgotten something and need to return to find it. My perennial return tickets demonstrate how I vacillate between the desire for home and the longing for freedom. I will never feel at home in one of the cities and the other constantly calls me, but not enough to make me move: I sit on the ground between two stools and read Magda Szabó's children's book *Tündér Lala* to the kids with a lump in my throat.

'What's up, Mama? Run out of breath?'

'Yes, darling.'

ↂ

On the last visiting day before the operation, a hot, lazy Sunday afternoon, the whole family got together at the Hospital in Amerikai Road to visit my father. They didn't allow young children on the wards and so we waited in the bare hall so that my sister's two older children could help my father down to the ground floor. I watched how they supported him on both sides, raising him a little at each step, because he was hardly able to use his legs. I wondered what this shy, sensitive girl and the boy who laughs a lot felt as they carefully helped the trembling old man to a chair. How different it must be for them, supporting him down the stairs, than it is for my sister and me, standing by the white wall, watching them from a distance, or for my mother, who is sitting obediently on the seat we pressed her into, calm and concentrated, registering his painfully slow progress in every nerve, as if she knew that there wouldn't be many more images of him to store away in her memory. And what does it mean to my father, now casting a slightly ashamed but grateful glance at these two attractive young people who have been so decent as to help him along his obstacle-strewn passage? What do children, grandchildren mean to him if they aren't comrades-in-arms or spiritual followers?

Having reached the ground floor, my father sank into the chair and gave us a smile of relief. Then he looked around with an expression as if to say: What's the matter with you all? We coughed in embarrassment, then embarked on an artificial conversation about the hospital and news of the insignificant world outside. My two small children snuggled up to me and studied my father from the safety of my body. Apart from not being able to walk, he didn't look particularly ill. Rather, he looked like someone who had woken late – which was not unusual, as he was by nature a night owl – and was only still in his pyjamas because he hadn't had a chance to wash. So we studied each other, my father on the chair, the rest of us crowded around our mother as if gauging how far we would have to leap if we wanted to cross from bank to bank on dry feet, when my son, Simon, suddenly took some firm steps over to my father and silently hugged him, before running back to us.

'Go on, you go over to your grandfather, too,' I encouraged my three-year-old little girl in a curiously weak voice. But she wouldn't budge. With the faultless intuition inherited from the female side of the family, she knew precisely why.

A child is a great gift in itself. Furthermore it can conduct the parent into real adulthood. When my sister's first little girl was born, I was hanging around with my father's old friend Gyuri Sándor among all the other excited visitors in the crowded corridor, trying to identify the newborn on the hospital TV's grainy screen.

'See, she has suddenly become more of an adult than we will ever be,' Gyuri said when he spotted my sister radiating happiness as she approached us down the corridor.

Now I understand what he meant, though I have no idea how he knew this. If you're prepared to do it, you can allow yourself the luxury of escorting your children through their childhood and so re-experience your own childhood through new eyes, with greater knowledge. A peep through the camera lens and there you are, a small, instinctive, messy creature with overwhelming feelings that completely fill you up, but now you can see what is happening around you. So far the camera has been on your shoulders, following every twitch of your body, but now it shifts to the corner of the room and is fixed there. From this new angle you see the big room of the nursery, the brilliant afternoon sunlight pouring through from one side, the polished glowing parquet, the children's faces flushed with happiness as they wait, their small, perspiring hands on knees, clad in blue tracksuit bottoms, sitting alongside each other on lined-up nursery benches, the table in the corner covered with goodies. Then you see the nursery teacher's lush head of hair grown pale through the use of cheap hair dye, her kindly smile as she leans to one side and produces from her sack a little devil instead of a Santa. Beyond the heart-wrenching terror, you see how the smile has never left the nurse's lips when she pretends to frown and asks in a deep voice: 'You there, tell me now, why were you so naughty on little Johnny Kádár's birthday?'

Maybe it wasn't little Johnny Kádár. Maybe no such person ever existed. But there was someone, a prominent comrade's important offspring, whose parents were upset because I had turned cartwheels on their son's birthday. They regarded my act as a provocation. And news of this provocation spread from the Saturday afternoon party through to nursery school on Monday morning, when I was duly told off at the very first group session. Three months later, when I waited in vain for my Christmas gift, I also understood that my crime was not just incomprehensible but imperishable. But now, with the aid of the corner camera, I begin to understand what must have happened. Now I am re-experiencing not only the shock and distress of a five-year-old – I was always a good girl! Always! – but also the nursery teacher's state of terror that led her to call the attention of the middle group to the question of my behaviour, at the Christmas party, months after the incident. And the startled silence of the group. At home I sobbed as I recounted why Santa had no presents for me this year. My mother tried to console me; my father, if he was told at all, would most certainly have explained it away.

To be honest, I had completely forgotten the Christmas incident. My childhood was, on the whole, happy and secure, and there were few comparable mishaps. For a while I tried to convince myself that the nursery teacher was wicked, but I couldn't maintain this position for long because she was good-natured and kind. After a time, I simply forgot the whole thing, chiefly because at the next nursery celebration I was treated according to my worth.

Certain memories slumber serpent-like in the folds of the brain until something disturbs them and brings them to life. The fence at Cinege Road nursery was like that. The image of it emerged from the long-buried past because of an incident with my daughter, who was by then seven. For the first time ever it had been arranged that her class should enjoy a few days in the mountains, a trip that entailed train journeys, boats and nights at tourist hostels. A couple of days before the party set out, when everything was in place, Róza announced to the class that she wasn't going. She resisted all questions, all attempts to charm her, all reasoning, with the most obstinate silence. Half the teaching staff were gathered round her by the time she finally hung her head and answered the teacher: 'I'm not going because you'll only leave me there.'

The teacher was so upset that she rang me and asked me to help. At home I went through every detail with my offspring and that was how, to my greatest surprise, I found myself by the fence in Cinege Road. Since my father was always occupied with the great Cause and my mother was constantly working, we spent much of our early childhood at the school crèche and most of the summer in various children's homes, until our parents could afford to take their well-deserved fortnight's holiday at one or other union holiday resort with the dizzy delights of food vouchers and organised entertainment. As a child, I had stood by the fence at the Cinege Road children's home, aware that the other children were orphans and that I was lucky not to be one of them, but all the same I spent hours standing there, with the portable radio in the neighbouring yard booming silly popular songs in the background, waiting for my mother to fetch me. My anxiety became overwhelming at times and I went to the carers in charge to say I was feeling ill. The children's home in Cinege Road was a real paradise: the carers smiled, the place was clean, there were masses of toys, an enormous jungle-like playground, and beds with bars set out on the terrace for our afternoon naps. But no amount of smiling carers or terrace beds could allay the ache at the pit of my stomach.

The following message soon arrived at the repository of Unsent Letters and Words Unsaid:

> Dear Szera,
> No need to return on the wings of nightmare. Now I know you were the fifth woman hovering about my father's bed. One day, when we find a flat we no longer need to leave we will have your photograph on the wall, too. The one in which you are walking by the lake, smiling, with your two children in tow.

A couple of days later, I suddenly had a thought, wrote the text down on a piece of paper and made a pretty paper boat of it. I took my children by the hand and we walked down to the lake. Carefully, we pushed the boat out on to the water and watched it as the waves swept it into the middle of the lake.

ᴓ

In retrospect, I had such a sunny childhood because reality and what my parents said about reality seemed in absolute agreement. At the beginning of the 1960s, the country started to come to life after the big freeze of its apparent death in 1956: survivors tentatively began to move their stiff limbs, and blood started on its wary circuit. The feeble light of reform was glancing through the system: it was possible to go to the cinema again and there was something to eat: what I never suspected was that we were sitting on a funeral banquette over the corpse of a strangled uprising. It was only a false dawn between 1956 and 1968, but there was enough faint sunlight to warm my childhood.

One Sunday afternoon at the end of the summer in 1968, we were visiting an old family friend, Auntie Rózsi, who was a doctor in a small village in the Danube Bend, that beautiful stretch of the river across from the town of Visegrád. On the way home, I followed my parents' anxious glances and saw how, on the rails beside us, ran an infinitely long series of tanks and green military vehicles, all heading north. We hurried home from the station and got into bed earlier than normal. We woke before dawn with dry throats, in dense darkness. As it turned out later, our lower-floor neighbour, crazy old Blanka, had made a fire in her stove and the smoke was being pushed back by the heat. Coughing, we felt our way out to the sitting room, where my mother had already opened the windows and was sobbing while trying to fan the smoke out. At first I thought that the smoke had got to her, but her tears continued to fall after the smoke had cleared. What's the matter? I asked her in fright, because it was the first time I had seen my mother crying. 'We've invaded Czechoslovakia,' she sobbed. 'And what does that mean?' I asked, even more frightened now. 'Does it mean we're at war?' 'It's like a war,' she answered, and sent us out to the balcony so that we would not be poisoned by the smoke. I gazed at the green chestnut tree below in shock and tried to grasp what it all meant.

For decades 1968 meant only the fright we had that morning, something that could be dispelled by airing the room. We generously forgave old Blanka and made jokes a long time after about why someone would choose precisely that hot August night to set fire to the past.

Some years later I no longer regarded Blanka as a mad old woman with a penchant for pyromania. When we were children, we tried to avoid her as far as possible because she had an unforgiving view of the world and barked at us whenever we spilt the ash from the ceramic stove that we had to clean every morning on the stairs. As I was to discover, she didn't make a racket only when neighbours spilt rubbish on the stairwell, but also in 1944 when they wanted to take away the Jews she was hiding, and in 1956 when they wanted to beat my uncle to death on account of his light tan shoes. It wasn't as if she cultivated communists, she just could not stand injustice. I listened to her for hours as a teenager, my neck growing gradually stiffer as I looked up at her perched in the upper-ground-floor window while she recited poetry or told me what it was like to be the first female medic at Szeged University and to roam Istanbul in the 1930s. Old Blanka's husband was another woman. Our neighbours in the house at Németvölgyi Road were typical twentieth-century Hungarian citizens who could display both the best and worst of humankind, switching between them at lightning speed, but nobody in the house ever dared curse her as a stinking pervert. I never discovered why she was so frightened on the night of the Czech invasion, but when she died, and when her companion committed suicide shortly afterwards, the upper-ground-floor flat remained for ever empty as far as I was concerned, whoever its new tenants were.

When I look at my children, what looks back at me is not only the 'me' of that age, along with her vanished world, but my child father, too. My little girl is seven years old now and my father cannot have been much older when they moved to Prague. Even if his parents didn't explain why they had to leave home, and even if the golden years of Prague followed, this must have been the first cloud in the carefree wide blue skies of his childhood. Through my two children, happily subsuming themselves in the discovery of the world, I can imagine what it must have been like for him to find one day his parents strangely tense and quiet, dismissing the beloved daily help, starting to pack, taking leave of relatives and close friends – most of whom, as we now know, they would never meet again – with an unusual stiffness, clutching the children's hands, while setting off on a long silent train ride at the end of which they would find themselves in an unfamiliar city, where people spoke an unfamiliar language, in unfamiliar schools and playgrounds, where the nine-year-old boy and the seven-year-old girl had to establish a place for themselves. No shots had yet been fired, no barbed-wired camps established, but Europe had sunk into a sinister silence and the age of innocence was over.

Primo Levi says somewhere that it was all those mountain hikes that saved him in the concentration camp. I don't know whether he meant the physical benefit or that incomparable feeling of freedom we discover on a mountain top, or at the edge of the sea, that gives us strength we may draw on once life narrows around us. But there were times on our happy excursions when the thought occurred to me that this might come in useful some time, as if the pleasure of taking deep lungfuls of fresh air and temporarily allowing myself to sink, without anxiety, into the arms of nature were not quite enough. It would be so much easier if I knew what world I was introducing these two gorgeous children to and from what terrible hellholes I might have to rescue them. But the way things are now, you can't get on a bus or a plane or enter a theatre without the thought that it might be precisely here, in this innocent-looking place, that a terminally embittered fellow member of the human race is waiting to spill your blood. On the altar of which sacred cause would you prefer to be sacrificed tonight, darling?

On the occasion of that memorable train ride on 19 August 1968, we were visiting Auntie Rózsi on the Danube Bend.

I was always a little scared of this gaunt, cold, stiffly formal woman. It might just have been her nature, but it might have been what happened to her that made her like that. In 1942 she and her husband arrived at the harbour in Amsterdam, clutching tickets for the next boat out, but at the very last moment she refused to go because she suddenly felt she could never live anywhere but at home, in Hungary. Two years later, her entire family was deported. In the spring of 1945 she walked back home from the concentration camp at Mauthausen to discover that she was the only survivor. She settled in a small village by the Danube and spent the rest of her time keeping the locals healthy by preventative treatment. Everyone else at the time thought the idea was ridiculous and Aunt Rózsi had to fight tooth and nail with both the medical authorities and her obstinate patients to be allowed to conduct her regular health checks. She married again in the early 1960s, but she could never forget the lanky young man whose death warrant she had signed in Amsterdam.

She was well past sixty when she decided to sign up for the evening course at the Marxist-Leninist university. Maybe she simply wanted to relieve her lonely evenings, maybe she hoped to gain a wider perspective on the narrow-minded bureaucrats she encountered, maybe she also wanted to understand better an ever more troubled world in which everything she once thought important was quickly vanishing. By the grace of good fortune, the person fate had appointed to be her tutor for the course of introduction was that assiduous spreader of the word, my father. It didn't take them long to find each other. Comrade Holló had within a few moments become the embodiment of truth, Aunt Rózsi's intellectual guide and spiritual support. Despite the stern front, all the passionate love that the elderly woman's murdered loves could never receive flowed like a torrent towards my father, who returned it with shy satisfaction and all-encompassing solicitousness. All the feelings for his own mother that he himself had thought buried for decades were directed towards this lonely old Jewish woman.

Years later, after a stormy summer night, feeling she was no longer strong enough to fight with the dark forces of destruction, stupidity and evil, Aunt Rózsi hanged herself in the attic above her surgery. She left her Budapest studio flat to me. At the beginning of the 1980s, a time of desperate housing shortages, this freehold flat was like a gift from the gods that freed me at a stroke from all the basic existential necessities that afflicted the great majority of my contemporaries, pushing them to make ever more bitter, ever more demanding human and professional compromises. I was perfectly aware that I gained my new freedom at the cost of someone else's suffering; I did not draw yet far-reaching philosophical conclusions from this fact, but I was enormously grateful.

ଔ

In his last days before the operation I was constantly waiting for my father to speak, to reveal something important about himself, to define his inheritance. But our intimate conversations, when they didn't concern his manuscript, consisted of minor banalities and we were often stuck for words. One day when the gaps in the conversation were unusually long, I asked him if it was difficult for him to speak.

'Yes, ever more difficult,' he said with mild panic in his eyes.

The havoc in his body was sending unmistakable signs to his brain but it seemed he was still set on ignoring them. I pulled from my backpack a thin book, Marguerite Yourcenar's *Oriental Tales*, that my friend Justine had brought me the day before I left Geneva.

'Would you like me to read some of this book to you?' I asked. 'I don't know what it's like, my friend lent it to me. But Yourcenar's a good writer, we can rely on her.'

My father nodded, relieved. I took the book and started to read. The story, based on an ancient Chinese legend, concerns the painter Wang-Fo and his students. Wang-Fo can paint so well that after a while people say his pictures come alive with the last stroke of his brush. The wealthy want him to paint guard dogs, the nobles want fully armed soldiers, priests regard him as a saint, and common people fear him because they are convinced that he can conjure up all kinds of terrible things. One dawn, soldiers drag Wang-Fo in front of the Emperor, who condemns him to death. His crime is that his painted world is more perfect than the real one where the Son of Heaven exercises absolute power. The world is nothing but a mass of scribbles a mad painter has committed to canvas, and our tears are always smudging it, says the Heavenly Dragon. As a last act of grace, the Emperor commands the old master to complete a half-finished picture that is kept in the palace. While the executioner heats his iron in the fire, Wang-Fo sets to painting the sky-high mountains, the waters of the sea and the clouds gathering at dawn. As soon as he moves his brush, the water breaks into waves and slowly covers the Emperor's palace. Soon a light little barque appears with Wang-Fo's faithful disciple, Ling, sitting in it. Under the astonished gaze of the courtiers, he helps the master into the craft and starts rowing. When the two disappear behind the cliffs on the horizon and the last plash of oars is heard, the water slowly withdraws from the palace. There are only a few damp patches left on the floor.

I don't know how far the words of Marguerite Yourcenar penetrated my father's tortured consciousness. He listened carefully and, whenever I glanced up at him, his eyes looked back, encouraging me to carry on. When I finished reading, I closed the book and gazed at him with a radiant smile as if to assure him that there would be consolation.

'You do a good job of translating,' said my father in his threadbare voice.

We sat quietly. I wondered if I should start another story or try some conversation. We were both looking at the tiles on the floor, smiling at each other occasionally. Soon my father said he'd like to rest. I drew the covers over him so he wouldn't be cold and crept out of the room.

The last night before the operation, I managed, once again, to sneak past the porter in his cabin and into the hospital. To my surprise, my father was sitting with Dr Cserjés on the white iron bed. They were quietly talking and there was something touching about the way they were leaning against each other, the doctor balanced, feet out, my father with his legs tucked under, as if afraid of sinking into the bed's worn wire webbing. As I panted my way in, Dr Cserjés stood up, adjusted his crooked brown tie and, after a few witty remarks, shook my hand and left. My mother was out in the corridor waiting to escort my father to the bathroom. We got hold of my father, who leant against us like a golem drained of all strength, and set off down the long corridor towards the showers.

On the morning of the operation, my sister and her husband picked me up at Németvölgyi Road and we drove to the hospital to see our father before he went into the theatre. My sister shouted at me because I wasn't ready in time, and she was right. I also knew how nervous she was and how she'd be weeping and screaming en route if she had her way as we moved through sluggish morning traffic in Alagút Street and over Lánchíd, the Chain Bridge. I shrunk into the back seat and watched people hurrying to work. When we reached the ward, my father was sitting on the side of the bed waiting for his operation. They had clearly given him a sedative, because he was a little dazed: he was happy enough to grasp our hands but found it difficult to speak. When the surgical assistant arrived with the trolley, my father seemed to fly into a mild panic like a traveller in a taxi who sets out on a long journey but is suddenly seized by the fear that he has left something behind. The envelope, the envelope, he kept saying as they loaded him on the trolley in their practised way and started wheeling him through the door. Once we were home, my mother explained that he meant the envelope of cash that we should have slipped into the assistant's pocket because paramedics are so badly paid.

My sister and I returned to the ward to pack our father's things. We were trying supernaturally hard to avoid an air of catastrophe. We might even have giggled at the great pile of handkerchiefs and newspapers by the bed, but then, when I happened to look up, through the window I saw his trolley being pushed along the short corridor to the operating theatre. I knew that the shape under the green covers was my father. For a moment I shuddered to think how quickly he had become part of another reality, part of an indifferent other system where he was no longer the father whose belongings we were gathering together with the gentle, mildly mocking affection of grown-up children, but a gravely ill man being wheeled to surgery, a tired body waiting for the knife.

We handed one of his suitcases in at administration so that he would be able to use what was in it while recovering from the operation, the other, full of books, manuscripts, brief notes on scraps of paper, newspapers already read and dirty washing, we took home, thinking they wouldn't be much use for a while. That suitcase stood for weeks in my father's vacant study, like an accomplice that had taken a mysterious role in the inevitable. I don't know which of us was brave enough to open it and allow its contents to merge with the predominant chaos of the study. But ever since then when I see the copy of Eric Hobsbawm's *Age of Extremes* on the shelf, I always remember it was the last book my father read with the unshakable confidence that he would at last understand why everything around him was falling apart.

The evening after the operation, I was sitting alone in the synagogue of the old people's home in Alma Street, in the dark office behind the window separating the praying menfolk from the women, and heard the sound of prayer filtering through it, staring through the bars on the window at a sky that was slowly darkening. I didn't know what to pray for. Dr Cserjés had talked of only three, at most six, months remaining for my father. That is if there were no new miracles. My mother and sister were, of course, waiting on precisely such a miracle. Having seen one, they mistakenly expected to see others. I sat in the growing darkness with empty thoughts rattling around my brain. I no longer expected a miracle, but to wish for anything else felt like murder. 'Don't let it. Don't let it be. Don't leave me here muttering like a fool. Don't leave me muttering like a fool when I'm about to meet my maker. A cat is sitting on my broken stove. Don't let it. Don't let me be sad.' I kept repeating to myself the mixed-up lines of Attila József's poem, like a cracked record, my needle stuck.

Sixth

The last time I saw my father alive, he was in intensive care, tied to his iron bed because he constantly wanted to rip out the tubes that were attached to him. While the children, who had been waiting outside the hospital gate with my sister, ran up and down the stairs stopping every so often to study the pattern of the wrought-iron railings, I stood beside my father in a dark green jacket, antiseptic gloves and wear-once-only slippers and tried to talk to him as he fought for breath. He could still talk when my sister, who was first, went in to see him, but my mother and I heard only fragments of words. I held his hand, gazing at the lilac patches where the infusions had been applied, and felt ever more desperate. 'I want to get out, I want to get out,' my father kept saying, and then he just gurgled. It was no use leaning over him, pressing his hand between my two palms; no point throwing a few words his way hoping he might catch hold of them. Before he finally lost consciousness for the last time his eyes looked far into the distance. 'I want to get out,' he suddenly moaned again and, gathering all his strength, shook the bed. That's his eternal yearning for freedom, my mythopoeic self might have said, but my mythopoeic self was squatting silently in the corner, unable to speak a word.

Saturday morning, two days after the operation, I was wandering back and forth between the kitchen and the hall of our flat in a dozier state than usual, preparing breakfast. My mother had been on the phone in the kitchen five times already describing father's pitiful condition in intensive care the previous night. When the telegram boy rang, I took the folded paper from him as in a dream and it was only after he'd galloped down the stairs that it occurred to me he would usually have waited for a tip. Why was he in such a rush? I asked myself as I shut the door. In the kitchen my mother kept talking to someone on the phone about the tubes my father had tried to tear out though his hands were taped to the bed. I placed the telegram on the table in front of her and went back to the hall, where the children were, to check whether they had succeeded in spilling milk all over themselves. Then I heard the terrible scream. My mother dashed about the narrow kitchen, incomprehensible cries bubbling up from her throat. I couldn't understand a word she was saying but my body ran chill from head to foot. She was flapping uncontrollably, like a bird caught in a cage, not knowing how to escape through the bars. She lurched against the fridge, against the corner of the table, against the entirely indifferent kitchen cupboard all the time screaming, and when she wasn't screaming she howled as if being beaten. I was afraid she'd hurt herself and tried to stop her, pouring a glass of water down her throat, but she snatched it from my hand and carried on floundering around in the kitchen. Hearing the great noise, Simon came in, his two enormous black eyes fixed on my mother, then, having seen enough, he turned on his heel and went back out again. My hand was shaking uncontrollably as I unfolded the telegram and smoothed it out:

> Dear Madam,
> We are sincerely sorry to inform you that your husband passed away on the ward at 4 this morning.

There might have been something else there, too, but these were the only words that kept ringing in my heavy head, each individual word like a dull stroke of the axe.

I tottered into the hall to check on the children. I bumped into little Róza in the corridor leading to the kitchen. She was busily trying to make her way out. There was a hastily drawn picture in red crayon in her hand.

'Look, Grandmother!' she said with the clear confidence of a three-year-old to my mother, who had somehow managed to leave the kitchen and was swaying around in the corridor. 'Here's Grandfather! Here he is! I have drawn him for you!'

My mother bent down to say something to the serious little girl who was gazing at her, but only faint squeaks rose from her throat. Róza pressed the drawing into her hand and fled into the children's room. Simon sat in the living room pressed right back in the deep armchair like someone forced into a corner.

'Mothers don't cry,' he pronounced staring directly at me. 'Mothers don't cry,' he repeated.

One part of my deeply confused consciousness had accidentally managed to hear what he was saying. I don't know whether it was an order or a plea, but it stuck with me.

Each time I tried to get close to my mother, she let out such blood-curdling wails I froze in terror. We circled each other in the flat, tottering around like people on a tempest-tossed boat. The children hid in their room. I stumbled into the kitchen to heat up the coffee that I had gone out for in the first place when the telegram boy rang. My hand was still shaking so I had to hold the cup in both hands not to spill the hot drink. Fortunately, my sister soon arrived and she dealt with the telephone calls that neither I nor my mother was capable of dealing with. A call from the hospital told us that this being Saturday there was nothing we could do regarding my dead father. As we looked at each other in astonishment, agony and horror it was immediately clear we had no idea how to come to terms with the new reality that had crashed in on us.

'I'm going to take a shower,' I said after a while.

Now that my sister had arrived I dared to leave my mother alone with her. My head was aching as if an enormous rock had fallen on it. All I could think of was that hot water would wash away all this absurdity. I stood very still under the steaming jet of the shower, surprised to see a long streak of red running down my leg.

'I'm going to take the children out for a walk,' I said to

my mother and sister huddling silently in the hall. 'You can discuss what needs to be done.'

We got on the 21 bus and took a ride to the hilltop. It was a crystal-clear summer morning, there were still heavy dewdrops hanging off the leaves of the trees which surrounded the playground. The children were happy they had the place to themselves. It was still very early in the morning. We weren't in the habit of arriving at the playground so early. By the time we got home, my sister had succeeded in getting my mother to take a tranquilliser. She was no longer a fluttering bird, but a robot. The children were starving after their busy morning. After lunch I put them down to sleep for a while, leaving the three of us to sit silently in the hall staring at the spines of the books. The ringing of the outside gate broke in on our silence. I went down to see who it was. The husband of my late friend Juli, who had died a couple of months before.

'I sense there's been some trouble,' he said.

'My father is dead.'

Having said it for the first time I was struck by the simple brutality of the sentence. We were standing at the doorway of the Németvölgyi Road house as I had done so often before, and with so many people: with childhood playmates who always escorted each other home, then later with friends, with lovers, with chance acquaintances and neighbours. Standing just like this, my back against the door that wanted to swing to and close, or in front of it, the key in my hand, listening to someone's story, or telling a story myself, saying simple things, passionate or bitter things, before the heavy gate through which whenever I pass I glance at the bullet holes on the metal cellar door right across the entrance – holes left over from 1956 and never repaired even when the entire house was renovated. I stood in front of the shut gate, the keys to the flat in my hands, my mouth uttering the words: 'My father is dead.'

'I thought so,' said Juli's husband.

Perhaps he knew because Juli was only two months dead and he genuinely mourned her, even though he would shortly have another woman at his side. Having spent a long time mourning in the empire of the dead, he might have sensed a new presence there. Possibly it's like the secret communication between babies: their eyes are always seeking each other out, registering the fact that there is another baby around; they recognise each other like people that have arrived from the same mysterious country, a country they still faintly recall. They can still speak the language of that country and abide by its laws, playing their – to us – incomprehensible yet systematic games. Maybe that is why those tiny creatures look at the world like wise old men; then this wisdom is slowly ground away by the loving family that tries to accommodate them to the demands of the world that now surrounds them. That is why it takes years for them to get used to it: learning is also a process of forgetting.

'Can I do anything to help?' asked Juli's husband.

'Thanks, I'll call you,' I said.

We hugged each other, then he limped back to his car. Only now did I notice that he had their dog with him. How often had Juli rested her hand on the dog's head as we were talking? It was shifting restlessly in the narrow passenger seat giving me accusing looks through the windscreen. I returned to the flat and we busied ourselves. I took the children to the playground again so my mother could have some peace. The children spent a lot of time in the fresh air that weekend. They were very amenable and were happy to go wherever I took them because they were scared of staying at home with my mother. Somebody had taken away the old grandmother and substituted a new one. The new one couldn't smile whatever you said to her, she just cried and didn't understand. Perhaps Grandmother was ill, too? Perhaps she too was going to die?

I have long known that truth is always discovered the day after. It's not in the throes of ecstasy but the next morning that truth arrives, when we first look at the figure sprawled on the bedcovers still heavy with dreams. The morning after moving in, the morning after separation, the first working day, the first kiss, the first failure, the first successful exam is the true measure of value. The point at which all-powerful weekdays claw back the time. The next day after my father's death was a Sunday. We were plenipotentiaries of time. There was no more need to run from place to place, to portion out hospital visiting hours, to decide who should look after the children; there was nothing we could do because official life was at a standstill. The corpses were patiently waiting to be dealt with while the living were hanging about at a loss in their suddenly empty lives.

On the Monday morning after my father's death we appeared at the office of the hospital in Amerikai Road with a set of his clean clothes. While my mother and sister dealt with the formalities, I stood in the corridor and tried to estimate how much the world had changed since my father died. Once all the paperwork was done, we sat our mother down on a vacant seat and my sister and I cut across the tiny yard to the mortuary to see our father's corpse. Mother didn't want to come. The talkative mortuary assistant ushered us into the office and went off, as he said, to prepare the body. What else was there to prepare? I wondered, as I sat in the chair by the desk, glancing distractedly at a copy of the sports daily and a pocket radio in its carrying case. My sister and I dared not look at each other. The fear that had overcome us might have been even stronger than the pain. When we were finally allowed into the cool chamber, there was my father lying on a white table, covered in a dark green blanket so only his face was visible. Warily, we drew nearer. The mortuary cavalier looked on the object of his work appraisingly.

'Can I touch him?' asked my sister.

'Go ahead,' the man replied.

My sister put her hand on my father's brow.

'How cold,' she said. The sense of awe at the physical wonders of the world barely covered the emotion in her voice.

I didn't dare touch him. I didn't even dare ask the assistant to turn back the blanket a little so I could see the childhood axe scar on my father's right hand. Perhaps I was afraid that I'd see traces of the efforts at resuscitation on his chest and so confirm the hospital reports of his struggle for life at dawn on Saturday. We stood in silence by the cold table. My father looked calm. There remained a slight, amazed smile on his face. It was as if, just before dying, he had been pleasantly surprised by something.

ଔ

Nineteen ninety-nine was a terrible year. In the spring the mother of my ex-partner, the man with whom I had lived during my post-university years before leaving for Mexico, died. She was a generous, frightened refugee from the past who still knew how to stick the knife blade into the soil so the knife would become kosher again, how to hand-sew buttonholes, and how to grow flowers from seed in yoghurt cups. On the Easter visit we both knew would be the last, we turned up my trousers, sewed the torn hook back on my coat, carefully packed the plants she gave me to plant on our Geneva balcony, tasted all the pastries specially baked for the occasion and exchanged what little news we had. Then we sat next to each other on the chequered couch, arm in arm, in silence. She wasn't scared, since she had so many people waiting for her on the other side, but the thought of the road there filled her with anxiety. We sat quietly on the couch and I kept staring at the clumsy chandelier hanging from the ceiling, something to yank me back into the ugly aesthetics of reality and prevent me from crying. Then we took a long, wordless goodbye, awkwardly hugging each other in the narrow hall that smelled of quince.

Juli was the next to die, my one-time classmate with whom I stopped every day at the doorway of the Németvölgyi Road house, because we had so much to say to each other that we had never managed to finish before I escorted her over to her flat in the block at Alkotás Road; with whom I experienced the great enthusiasms of childhood and the first glittering passions of adolescence. Eventually we drifted apart, but each time we met the spark of genuine affection was re-lit. I hadn't the least notion that she would die at forty-seven. The day that she was between two blood transfusions, fighting for her life, I happened to be returning to Geneva from a conference in London. Brimming with impressions, I stood exhausted under the pitiless light of the airport washroom examining my face in its mirror. I saw the skin sagging around my eyes, the hair slowly fading above my brow and the tiny lines that formed a delicate web at the corners of my mouth. Well, well, am I getting old? I asked myself morosely, but then I had to run to catch my flight. Later in the evening when, blanked out by exhaustion, I sat down in front of the computer to see what I had missed I found a short e-mail from her husband saying that she had died that afternoon.

The others who died: My friend Tamás's father. The father of my old schoolfriend Dobó. My university friend Ilona's father.

Fathers die early here. Perhaps they have had too much of history. Too much revulsion piling up in their heads, crushing their spines, scrambling their brains, breaking their hearts. Mothers survive better.

❧

The ten days between the death and the funeral were filled with another bout of feverish activity. The telephone was constantly ringing: settling affairs, funeral arrangements, lawyers, mother, children, relatives. People tiptoed around us as though we were carrying some serious infectious disease. One day we returned to the hospital because, in the chaos following our seeing the corpse, we had left behind the suitcase prepared for my father's convalescence. I vaguely remember a long walk with Miki Winter and, like suddenly coming upon an island at ebbtide, the surprise appearance of my long-unseen Dutch friend Magda in the hall of the Németvölgyi Road flat.

On the rare occasions when I was alone, all my thoughts revolved around my father's mysterious, inconceivable departure. I still hadn't recovered from the shock that something so important should have occurred while our backs were turned. It was no use our father being part of our lives if he escaped us at the last moment and died among strangers, far away. Just as we had not really been partners in his life, so we had not been 'invited' to his death. I was, at the same time, overwhelmed by an all-consuming sense of guilt. We left him to die alone in a bare hospital bed abandoned between night and dawn.

There was not a moment's relief from my headache ever since my father died. Medicine, walking, coffee, cold showers – nothing would shift it. I swayed from one task to another, my head splitting. I felt every last ounce of my strength was taken up in the fight against pain. One day I was seized by a terror: this can't be normal; there must be something wrong with me. Ah, now I understand. This is it! He's here and I'll go to the grave with him. Help! He's a vampire! He so didn't want to die he wanted to change places with me, but he was late, as always, and now he's trying to drag me with him. Help! Help! Dr Cserjés, please cut this pain from my head because I can't stand it any more.

☙

In the first few days after my father died we discovered that his study was full of perishable items we had no idea were there and it urgently needed cleaning. In the previously locked drawers of his desk, in spaces between the wall and items of furniture, behind disciplined rows of books, the clutter of his life lay before us. Books, newspapers and notes going back several years were carefully arranged in heavy piles; we found stale chocolate and bits of carefully wrapped food; there were bottles of cognac, at least twenty litres of mineral water, empty jam jars, various sizes of plastic bags and first-aid kits, dozens of long-dried wet wipes (the kind they distribute on air flights), several rolls of loo paper, carefully hidden presents for a wide range of family and friends, remains of unsent letters and stacks of letters received, piles of paper with notes, poems (poems?!) neatly tied together with string, the last of which was written on the occasion of Gyuri Sándor's death. There was a whole pile of stuff that 'might come in useful some time', including cutlery from the Soviet Union and torches from China; there were thirty years' worth of manuscripts, files of diploma works and doctoral supervisions complete with my father's own detailed notes, and a vast number of laundry and household bills, including some with scribbled notes on the back. While we were trying to bring some order to this overwhelming stock of material, I felt my father was still present in the study. Or perhaps it wasn't him but someone else who just looked like him. One day we discovered a photograph of him standing on the balcony with my sister's two-week-old first child: I had never seen his face like that, radiating so much happiness.

My father's study was a survivor's island, fitted out with all kinds of long-term provisions. But what was there to survive ten, twenty, thirty, forty years after the war had ended? Was it a deep-seated fear that told him to be ready to run, since they might come at any moment with their loud boots and yelping dogs or, some years later, without the dogs but in silent black cars and plain clothes, treading lightly this time, to ring the doorbell in the middle of the night and take him away as they did so many others? Was it the dark shadow that could be waiting at any time behind the glazed front door of our flat, ready to sweep away in one gesture everything he considered firm and stable? Were these supplies necessary in case there was bombing, or a siege, or in case they turned off the water or the electricity, poisoned the air, or were looking to starve him out? They might be here already, breathing heavily out in the hall among the books. The bed must be ready to block the door. A person could survive on what had been accumulated here until the rescue teams arrived – for weeks, perhaps.

Seven days after my father's death the various clocks positioned all over the flat, all showing different times – because there was never a precise time at Németvölgyi Road – started chiming. I was on my hands and knees in my father's study, filling the latest of God knows how many sacks with hard-as-concrete sandwiches and tins long past their best-before dates, when one of the alarm clocks started screaming. After a little while a Soviet-produced clock, complete with a now defunct thermometer, also began to ring, and then a third that I couldn't even see because it was covered in manuscripts somewhere behind me. I got into a terrible panic. I had no idea what momentous event had set all these clocks ringing: what was about to begin or end. What to do? Where to run? What spell to mutter in order to snatch back my father from the void at the last possible moment?!

☙

I don't know what my father would have said had the angel of death offered him a choice of different kinds of death. That is assuming a person can make choices about place of residence, life partner, death. People killed in the concentration camps had not just their lives but their deaths taken from them, the personal and individual death that is constructed in the course of a person's entire life and is a part of it. The death factories of totalitarianism worked on a mass scale and were for ever inventing more efficient methods. Concentration camps and nuclear bombs emerged from the sleeves of mass production, from methods of production that had lost their rational purpose. At one point the self-perpetuating holy trinity of mass production, mass consumption and mass culture set out on its terrifying triumphal march, when the art of making qualitative distinctions was pushed aside in favour of the religions of speed and unlimited output. People in the camps did not suffer individual death; not even their death was their own. A person deprived of all personal characteristics, of a past, of loved ones, of a home, of all of life's references, is dead before he enters the gas chamber. And this industrialised, neutral mass butchery strips away the value of life even in retrospect. If nothing, no character, no values, no merit could impede that death, if life was so easy to take away, then it was utterly worthless.

Maybe my father's death 'in bed, among pillows', as Petőfi put it some years before he was killed on a battlefield in the 1849 war of independence, was not majestic enough for the messianic faith that impregnated his life. But was it possible to dream of meaningful life and majestic death after the death camps? Was it still possible to think of a letter of farewell from the shadow of the gallows that would serve as an inspiration for posterity for decades? Was my father still longing for a hero's death like that of his childhood idols, those shining rebels Garibaldi, Marat and Petőfi? Did he ever imagine what Petőfi might have felt as he tried to escape the riders pounding across the heroic fields of Segesvár in pursuit of him? What raged in his heart, the euphoria of perfect sacrifice or blind panic? When he heard the horse's hoofs drumming right behind him, then stop for a moment as the horse rose on its hind legs so the descended blade might strike with greater momentum, when he felt the edge of the cold blade enter his flesh that was still hot from running, was he then glad that he wasn't dying 'in bed, among pillows'? And when he was lying among the high yellow corn, his face swimming with salty sweat, did he think that perhaps General Bem, who tried to keep him away from the battlefield, might have been right after all? That life, this unpredictable, transient piece of magic, was after all worth more than the terrible, pointless death that was about to overtake him in the next few moments; that the heroic death so honoured and lauded in school textbooks was only a dry throat, a choking pair of lungs and eyes starting in terror, and blood, filth and loneliness.

In the nervous half-hour before the burial, wc gathered in the upper section of the Németvölgyi Road cemetery near the Hóvirág Street entrance. We had left the children with my friend Márti. They didn't complain: it was as if they knew that it might be best to steer clear of the day's events. My father lay on the bier in his best black suit, white shirt and tie, but without shoes. The funeral director advised us to take the shoes back with us as they'd be stolen otherwise. My mother had placed a small notebook and pen in his right-hand top pocket so he could carry on making notes in the other world. Speak, Charon! Tell me about your life story, the conditions of your dwelling and the fate of your children. And how about your social background and work experience? And what did it all amount to?

My father lay obediently in his coffin. In the ten days since his death he had shrunk into a defenceless old man. His eyes were sunken, the joyful little smile on his lips had vanished and he seemed to be frowning as he waited to see what would happen next. He looked a little like Lenin, whose embalmed body we were privileged to glimpse on one occasion, having waited for several hours in the vast Red Square where the endless queues wound and crossed each other. This time I was brave enough to look for his childhood scar, the souvenir of his accident with the axe. It was there on his right thumb. Lost in thought, I gazed at his still hand, laid carefully next to his body. It looked as if it was clad in a small, horn-coloured glove. I glanced at his face, looked back at the glove and came to the conclusion that my father, the great fugitive from death, had found a new secure hiding place.

The state funeral service did not seem fully in control of the situation. There was some confusion with wreaths and, after the speeches and some initial crackling, we found ourselves with the middle of the letter aria from *Tosca*, '*E lucevan le stelle*', coming at us with such power I thought it would burst the eardrums of everyone present. The second time they managed to find the beginning of the track, and Giuseppe di Stefano's tenor voice soared and settled on the dark mass of mourners like a soft, light black veil. A poem by Neruda was recited by my friend Judit, who had just recovered from cancer and was wearing a sexy black mini-dress, her smile as dazzling as if we were at a christening. For a moment the hands of the Party comrades who were distributing leaflets at the back trembled at the sight of her bold décolletage.

As I scanned the ranks of familiar and unfamiliar faces, some I hadn't seen since childhood, I was humbled by the sheer number of people who had come all this way in the stifling heat to pay their respects to my father. The family was lined up behind the coffin like prisoners awaiting execution. Poor Steven stood behind me shifting from foot to foot. I could sense him thinking tensely: Good heavens, are these people about to start rending their garments? The dark hall floated in front of me with its miserable artificial lighting, while the sun blazed in triumph outside. The black-clad sweating bodies seemed to melt together in the heat. Faces blurred in front of my eyes. I found my lips muttering quiet courteous responses as I stood up straight, clutching my mother's arm like someone fated from birth to stand like this for ever. I strained my every sinew to make sure everything went smoothly, so she wouldn't faint, nothing would be forgotten, there would be no mishap. It was only when I saw my friend Magda's face harden with grief that I realised that I, too, was involved in this, that the helpless weight in the dark brown wooden coffin was my father waiting to take up his last lodging in the Németvölgyi Road cemetery.

'It's only his body,' I muttered to my mother through my teeth as we stepped stiffly uphill, like wooden puppets, following the car bearing the coffin.

I noticed how one of the gravediggers spat in his palm before thrusting his spade into the pile of earth, then, with beautiful, regular movements, started to fill the hole. I was relieved the speeches were over and that no one had anything more to say: you could see the gravediggers were in a hurry as there was another funeral procession waiting behind us. The thought occurred to me that, had not my father refused to be a Jew even in death, his body might have found itself among some good friends further down the cemetery, in the Jewish section. But children's graves and enormous trees are not such bad company after all, I thought, and kept staring at his name with incomprehension. What was this name that was written on the front door to our apartment doing here on a label nailed on a yellowish strip of wood stuck into a pile of earth.

After the burial, the family got into a car and drove home. Back in Németvölgyi Road we sat in the living room with the blinds down on account of the heat. In the oppressive silence my uncle Mihály suddenly produced a bottle of something alcoholic and started to tell an incomprehensible story in a cracked voice. Immediately everyone livened up and we fell over each other with stories about the dead man; we offered each other drinks in the dead man's glasses; we shouted and laughed, drunk on the dead man's liquor, drunk with the proximity of death, drunk on sheer despair; we were laughing so much that we had to lean against each other to support ourselves. My mother sat motionless in the middle of the room, as if completely deaf to our unruly noise.

Back there in the silence and heat of the cemetery, a black-suited man wearing a kippa was bowing over the grave. It was Miki Winter, once the leader of the Endre Ságvári young pioneer troop and the first great love of my life.

The days after the funeral were leaden and slow. My sister joined her family on holiday, unable to bear the flat with its deathly closeness. My mother and I busied ourselves with things that had lost their meaning. In the evenings, once the children were asleep and my mother was not crying so much, we talked about my father. It was as if we wanted to fix him in our memories while his presence and absence were still fresh. The image the two of us arrived at was probably the closest we ever got to my father's complex and contradictory personality.

But beyond grieving together we also had to come to terms with our individual loss. Once we parted, we vanished into our separate dimensions: my mother into despair; myself into a void. I lay on the bed with open eyes. My head was a numb emptiness in which thoughts flew about like specks of dust in the sunlight. Sometimes I felt pain, at other times I was prey to a host of unanswered questions. In order to control the pain, I occupied myself with logical speculation, on the assumption that once I could explain things I could fill the hole left by my father's departure. I tried to number the factors that determine the kind of death waiting for us unannounced around the corner, while we are still full of our everyday thoughts. Could my father have lived a different life? Could he have broken the ties that bound him to communism? Did he have any choice in the matter? I thought about the Polish theatre critic Jan Kott and the economist Joseph Stiglitz, both of whom underwent dramatic changes in their lives. Their examples showed that early commitments are not necessarily lifelong. But what does it take to bring about such a radical conversion? Courage, honesty, accident, vanity?

My father's self-defence mechanism was in perfect order; he tried to ignore, deny or rationalise away anything that might lead him to question his faith. It speaks well of him that he lied, but wasn't cynical; he tried to hand on only those lies in which he himself believed. The trouble was that by erecting such powerful defences he did not see that he was losing the chance of development.

In the farewell letter he wrote before his first operation, when he still had the strength to write farewell letters, he claimed that he had not lived in vain. By his own lights therefore he was happy. So why did I want him to account for himself?

One night it struck me that it wasn't my father I was mourning, but the person he might have been. I thought he had failed to realise his true self, but that the possibility remained in him right to the moment he died. Under that badly cut commissar suit there was an old-fashioned humanist patiently waiting to emerge. It was the weight of two deaths that had settled on me.

When it was our turn to take a holiday, the evening before we left, I opened the door to my father's study and looked around. I had the strange feeling that he was still there. He might still be hiding, who knows in what form, among those thousands of unopened, unread notes and letters, among that pile of things, in that overwhelming saturation. I quickly closed the door behind me and started searching. Everything was as we had left it in the last rush of tidying; now it was possible to get to the window without tripping over too many obstacles on the way, and nor did the heaps of books look like they were about to collapse. I leaned against the bookshelves and took a deep breath. It didn't matter that my father had been buried for ten days, I could still smell him in his study. The next time I would return, the chaos – more manageable, perhaps – would still be here, but this smell, the characteristic smell of his living body that had permeated everything in the room: that would be gone.

The greater part of his books and notes remain where they were to this day. We drank the bottles of mineral water and distributed the more expensive drinks among doctors and plumbers. Items that 'would come in useful one day' actually did come in useful and, if they didn't, we discreetly threw them away. My mother's brothers inherited most of his clothes, while the polo-neck jumper bought for his birthday but never given to him passed to my friend Tamás and his knitted waistcoat went to Miki Winter. I brought the only top-quality shirt with me to Geneva and gave it to a friend's husband whose own father had been working for the Red Cross and had been killed in the Liberian civil war by a stray bullet. My friend's husband was so taken aback by my gesture that he avoided me for some time – a good example of the kind of Genevan tact I sometimes ramble on about.

When my sister arrived back from her holiday and started re-arranging life with her usual energy, we went away to the small Greek village where we took our regular summer vacations. My mother was unwilling to move from the flat. The plane touched down late at night. We got into a taxi, I wound the window down, the children leaned against me and immediately fell asleep. The taxi's engine struggled loudly up the hill as I gazed out at the scented silence and asked myself why I wasn't feeling anything. Where was the annual joy that used to fill me as we passed each familiar village, olive grove, bend of the road, each familiar house and hedge? I felt the breeze and the fresh air mingled with the smell of vegetation; heard the noise escaping lighted inns; noted the wayside trees caught in the circle of the headlights, the dry earth under the wheels, the brilliant starlit sky and there, over the hill, like a secret promise, the endless velvet darkness of the sea. Good to arrive, I sighed to myself, but I might never be as happy as before. I might never again be astonished by the way the afternoon sun illuminates the olive groves, opening a secret door into another world; unable to lose myself in the delicate web of green fern leaves or in the never-ending music of cicadas. I might never again watch, enchanted, as the children play their mysterious games, smile at the transparent rituals of flirtation on the beach, or be moved when the waiter in the out-of-the-way fish restaurant comes straight over to shake my hand. Will I ever be happy again walking on my favourite old paths, discovering a half-eroded inscription on a crumbling gateway, feeling the sea stroke my skin, hugging the old woman in her black scarf, breathing in the heavy scent of flowers in the evening? Will I sit again on the balcony admiring the brilliant Milky Way? Will I make love again for the pleasure of it, not just to prove, despairing lump of flesh, that I am still alive?

After the anxiety of the first few days had passed and I felt at home again, I was surprised at how tranquil I felt. It was good to be the familiar outsider in the cliff-top house, the foreigner who visits every summer wearing the same sun-faded dress, the same dusty sandals, the same decomposing straw hat, walking along with her family on a boiling hot day, greeting passers-by with a hearty hello, a nameless statistic in a place whose laws and regulations are as much a mystery to me as my world's are to them. The sleepy little village we stay in each summer is a small universe of which we become a part in our holiday weeks, the part we have paid for, a part just long enough to let the time allotted pass with as little disturbance as possible. We turn off the Calor gas flasks, draw down the blinds and go for a swim. We greet the locals. When we pack up at the end of summer there is no trace of us left in the house, nothing preserves our memory. The owners throw away the stones we carefully gathered on the beach, and the villagers may occasionally mention us in the long damp winter months, but they can't quite recall our names and if we didn't turn up one summer, someone else would take the house.

It doesn't hurt to be an outsider here. On the contrary, it is a kind of protection, especially this particular summer. I don't have to look sad, I don't need to show what I feel. As the days pass, everything gets simpler. We don't have to make life-changing decisions: all we have to decide is whether to turn left or right to the nearest sandy beach. We save our energy to attend to the essentials: the changing colours of the sea, the path of the sun, the secrets of the night, the twisted trunks of the olive trees and the billowing of silvery-blue dragonflies.

But two weeks later, on the point of leaving, I suddenly feel a new wave of sadness. I remember my father: it isn't an overwhelming flood of feeling this time, more a kind of regret that I can no longer ask him simple questions, like why he drank his coffee without sugar, when precisely did he have that accident with the axe, or what street did they live on in Prague? I regretted it, because I had been too busy with big questions that I insisted he should answer, even while knowing that I would have to solve them for myself without his help. I realised suddenly that the fact that he was no longer a moral or political compass, that he was growing ever less significant to people, might have played an equally important role in my father's death as the wildly growing number of diseased cells in his brain.

The last time I turned to my father for an answer was probably when, on one of my autumn visits, we went to the typist. He could still walk pretty well and he made his way up Goldmark Károly Road without too much trouble. We were taking something to be typed up, because he never learned to use the small laptop I had bought him for his great new work and he always remained dependent on others to produce a presentable hard copy of his chaotic manuscripts. Fortunately there was still one warm-hearted typist left over from the old days who had an out-of-date electronic typewriter, and who was willing to type up his scrawly longhand, full of emendations, excisions and stuck-on notes, working hard to decipher the more incomprehensible parts. We were walking down Határőr Road, towards the cogwheel railway, when I asked him whether it was an inevitable part of adulthood to feel permanently that everything is crumbling around us. It was worse before the war, he said, and his answer comforted me in a strange way. In that case destruction is just the usual way of things, I told myself, not realising that I had just broken with one of our most important principles: an optimistic view of human progress.

I took my leave of the sunny island and the warm sea, packed all my family's belongings into the big black suitcases and we set out on the journey back to the calm, ordered and measured city of Geneva where, unlike in Budapest, my father's absence did not shout at me from every street corner.

ꝏ

Summer ends all of a sudden in Geneva: one moment it is there, the next it is gone. The temperature drops abruptly and it begins to rain unendingly: the light sandals, the thin summer dresses immediately vanish into the dark winter prison of the clothes trunk, even though our bodies protest, hoping that some good weather will return, an Indian summer, with the sun stroking us one last time before we face again the icy wind. There may be days of brilliant sunshine, but it is an autumnal sun that we enjoy, wearing pullovers and proper shoes, and it is for our eyes only, not for our whole beings. The summer my father died ended in Geneva as abruptly as if it had been cut with a knife. We dressed in heavy clothes and wore solemn expressions. School started. We worked according to precise routines, reacquainted ourselves with the hard task of getting up early.

My father's death excused everything. When the children shrank from strangers, when I found myself ringing home all the time, when I didn't finish my work to the given deadline, it was my father's fault for dying. Autumn produced its usual fruits: pears, apples, full-bodied grapes, a second generation of strawberries. The trees by the lake wore purple and gold. I wasn't in mind-bending agony, just numb with anxiety for my mother. I still leapt with fright each time the phone rang. Death was the constant presence in everything I did.

In mid-October I called on Dr Vesely for the usual homeopathic prescriptions against winter colds. Dr Vesely was a surgeon and our local practitioner. Energetic and intelligent, she was a formidable figure. Apart from the normal medical qualifications her passionate interest in the human body had led her to diplomas in traditional Chinese medicine and acupuncture. One morning, years before, when I rang her on account of a persistent bout of bronchitis, her normally cheerful voice sounded rather hollow. When I asked what was the matter, she told me, after a brief hesitation, that her thirteen-year-old daughter had had an accident and was still in a coma after two months. The girl eventually emerged from the coma with the consciousness of a two-year-old child, screamed with pain for a whole year, then died. She was the second child Dr Vesely had lost. Her first had died of cancer at the age of three.

'At the time I thought nothing worse could happen to me,' said Dr Vesely. 'As if one could make deals with pain.'

Dr Vesely had married a Czech man, which might have helped her to understand the tormented Eastern European soul slightly better than had she married into a regular Genevan Calvinist family. All I know of this man is that he had had to flee Czechoslovakia when our comradely tanks invaded and that, even after the resounding loss of two children, he, like my own dear father, was unwilling to look death in the eye.

When I appeared for my autumn visit to the surgery, after the customary courtesies, Dr Vesely did her usual check-up, found everything to be all right and then, after looking at me again, asked what was that enormous rock over my head.

'My father died,' I told her.

I quickly recounted the circumstances. She looked at me thoughtfully, then suggested we arrange a brief ritual through which I could take leave of my father. I was a little taken aback, but nodded automatically as I did to everything she suggested. Dr Vesely told me what should be done. The ritual would consist of three parts. In the first I would say out loud everything I loved about my father and our relationship. In the second I would say what I didn't like. In the third I would go through all that I had inherited from him, everything that, because or in spite of him, had become part of my life. After this was done I should imagine an infinity sign, with my father in one loop of it and myself in the other. Then I was to cut the link between them.

Some weeks later I caught the bus to the surgery. Dr Vesely laid me down on the bed where she normally administered acupuncture and, as if nothing could be more normal, opened the floodgates. I was embarrassed at first because I found it hard to get over the absurdity of the situation: here I was in a foreign city, lying on a couch in a surgery, with a near stranger beside me in the fading sunlight, speaking to a dead person in an incomprehensible language. But once I got through the first few minutes, I was surprised how naturally one thing followed another. After a little while I sensed my father crouching in the dim yellow light, in the left-hand corner of the surgery. He was there without his usual defences, more real than I had ever seen him. After the initial heart-in-the-mouth feeling I spoke to him without fear or caution, in a way I had never done before. In the torrent of liberated words and feelings there was a moment when I heard the shuffling of paper and a gentle noise like a pen quickly passing over a smooth page. Poor Dr Vesely, she must have had quite enough of this and was writing up her medical notes, I thought. Perhaps it was a prescription she was writing, or an instruction that I should be removed immediately to the nearest locked cell? But then my thoughts returned to my father, who was still squatting in the left-hand corner of the room. We were at the third stage of the ritual now, where I was to say what mark my father had left on my life. Once I had finished, I listened in exhaustion as Dr Vesely spoke again.

'Now imagine the infinity sign with you in one loop and him in the other! Then cut the link between the loops.'

I saw the infinity sign with my father in one loop and a shape in the other that might have been me. I waited a while trying to understand what kind of space we were occupying. When I looked over to him, my father was still there, unmoving, his whole being clinging on to life. I waited a while, then started to speak again. 'You can go now,' I said. 'No one will threaten you there. There'll be neither shame nor pain. You don't need to fear anything any more'.

I spoke quietly, patiently, like someone persuading a child to put on his raincoat so he'd not be soaked to the skin. After a while I felt my father was no longer in the room. But he hadn't left, he had simply been absorbed slowly into the available space: he'd turned to water. I've no idea why specifically water. Perhaps so that he might remain among us a little while longer because in our worldly lives we had always been water monsters, always settling by some river or lake, always dreaming about the sea. For a fortnight or so after that I continued to feel his presence in the lake, then he vanished for good.

When, tearful and covered in perspiration, I sat up and tried to pull my body together, I saw Dr Vesely sitting perfectly politely behind her desk. For a while we looked at each other in silence.

'He didn't want to go,' I said at last.

'And?' she asked.

'I had to persuade him.'

'And then?'

'Then he slowly dissolved into water.'

'What water?'

'I don't know. All kinds of water.'

I stood up weakly, my muscles trembling. The rock did not hang over me any more.

'He has left this message for you,' said Dr Vesely and gave me a scrawled prescription. My hands were shaking so much I couldn't have read it even if her writing were legible.

'I can't read it,' I grunted.

Dr Vesely took the slip of paper back and read it to me. My father had responded to everything I had said in the ritual, item by item, and then he had said farewell. Now he was letting me go my way, wishing me the best. I stared at Dr Vesely.

'But how did he say all this?' I stuttered. 'Did he learn French after he died?'

'I don't think so,' she laughed. 'There are other forms of communication. From soul to soul.'

This was too much for my tortured brain, brought up on dialectical materialism. I felt I should escape immediately, before Dr Vesely started reciting the entire volume of Árpád Tóth poems, *From Soul to Soul*. My legs were about to buckle.

'Aha! Ha ha! Ha ha ha! Ha ha, ha ha!' I started laughing hysterically.

We smiled at each other blissfully. Then, forgetting the Swiss medical code of practice, she took a couple of steps, embraced and kissed me, then helped me out of the surgery. It was evening and dark by then. I made my way home down the deserted streets as if lost in some strange town. For a while I followed cars' headlights, then the constant mingled noise of the traffic. Suddenly I felt the ground vanishing from under my feet and had to sit down on a cold stone bench to recover my strength. After a long while I stood up cautiously and set off again.

I seemed to have been wandering in the dark for hours when I finally saw the lake. I gave a relieved sigh. There was a refreshing breeze blowing on the bridge. I looked down and gazed at the black water, a dark maternal presence, far from home, but still a landmark.

When, a couple of months later, I told my mother about this visit, she listened attentively and assured me that the piece of paper full of scribble in my possession was a proof of Dr Vesely's remarkable perception and psychological skills enabling her to put my mind at rest.

ꕥ

My beloved sister,
To pick up on our earlier conversation. What matters is not what he gave, or what he wanted to give us, but what we received. In any case, what people choose to leave and what we really inherit are two different things. One of Simon's most important memories is of Father reading the story of Moses to him. I know what lay behind this distinctly formative element in his life: Father was left alone with his grandson for an hour, but had not the least idea of what to do with a five-year-old child. The simplest thing was to hide behind a book and communicate with him in that way. Since they had already read the dinosaur book that was on the top of the pile several times, he grabbed the book under it and conscientiously read it from cover to cover to my bright-eyed little boy. It told the story of Exodus and of how Moses had gone to Mount Sion to get the Tablets of Law. It was a big book, with colourful illustrations, that had emerged from the permanent flow of things at Németvölgyi Road; I have no idea how it got there. Whether by heavenly decree or by blind chance and circumstance but certainly despite himself and quite against his own wishes, Father presented his grandson with one of his most important early experiences and revealed what he most wanted to hide: the fact that he was a Jew.

Love
Y

ଓ

Dear Miki,
A short while ago I discovered that my father was born on the same day many years after Ignác Goldziher. This must be the utterly scientific explanation for my overflowing love of Persian civilisation. Last week I saw an exhibition of Persian art of the last seven thousand(!) years. There were a couple of stunning miniatures, some wonderful gold artefacts, some gorgeous ceramics and the account books of Xerxes graven on stone. But what moved me most was a tiny cream tub made of that deep blue material that was only manufactured in the East. The tub was being held by an owl with a sad, knowing expression on its face, as if it were saying: 'Make yourself pretty, my dear, since life, for all your beauty and charm, is as brief as the beating of a wing.' I shuddered as if someone had suddenly greeted me. From the depths of a forgotten past someone had said something perfectly contemporary and conversational. It's the kind of thing that happens when you read Rumi's poetry, when you start to suspect that the translator has smuggled in your own worries and thoughts.

In one room there were pictures of long-vanished cities projected on to the wall to the sound of classical Persian music. I sat in the darkness listening to the sound of the kamancheh, staring bewitched at the images that passed before me. Just as our bodies retain the memory of our traumas and pleasures, so the earth absorbs and preserves the traces of people as they follow each other: ruins of streets and houses that are now hills and mountains, regular geographical features. The past is gone for ever, but from a certain height we can see that it was once the present and that there are traces of it all around us.

I would have stayed there for hours but the attendants

politely ushered me out. I bought a catalogue – I'll show it to you in the summer.

Love
Y

P.S. Regarding birthdays, I discovered among Gigi's notes that I was born on the same day as Szera, my grandmother. Imagine how many forms my father must have filled out listing the birth dates of his mother and his daughter, without ever saying anything to me about it.

Seventh

One grey morning in the autumn following my father's death, on Yom Kippur, when I was still in mourning, I was walking through town, deaf and blind, simply a robot fulfilling all the tasks required of me. The pain was not as heavy as it had been, it was rather as if I was wrapped in a thousand layers of aluminium foil, so that I would not fall apart or feel anything. I followed my routine mechanically: bathroom, wardrobe, kitchen, stairs, lift, peeling paint on walls, grey morning street, look left, look right, a small hand in mine, my only contact with the living. Nursery, hop on the bench, off with the shoes, on with the slippers, '*Bonjour, bonjour*', newsagent's, baker's, post office. This time a letter to pick up. A faintly familiar handwriting on the small blue envelope.

I left the post office deep in thought. I certainly felt that I knew that handwriting, but had no idea whose it was. My mind was still focused on the blue envelope and the half-recognised postmark, trying to work it out, but my heart was already racing and suddenly I felt unbearably hot. I hadn't opened the letter yet but, by the time I reached the shore of the lake, I knew who it was from and had to sit down on a cold stone bench to read it. I took great care opening the envelope: it was as if the letters were made of glass and the merest knock might shatter them. The text spoke of years and distances, of a new job, a new life and a grown-up child trying his luck in America. And about my shadow that had flitted across a good many evenings, across 'mistaken greetings and unfinished letters torn into a thousand tiny pieces'. Who knows how long I stayed sitting there on the damp bench. When I finally managed to stand up and look at the sky, a window had opened in that desperate mass of grey and an invisible hand had written a character on the surface of the lake.

חי

Life

The figure that suddenly emerged on that grey autumn morning from the fog of dreams, yearnings and memories after a thirteen-year absence was the second great love of my life. If we are lucky we are granted one true love in life, a romantic old man once told me; he having found his just a few months before he died. For me there were two. You little Stakhanovite, always over-producing, muttered the socialist realist in my head. I'm sorry, I inherited it from my father, I answered modestly. Yes, but which of the two was the real one? quibbled the eminent hair-splitter. Both,

I answered, but then I remembered my father making his way down the spinach-coloured corridors of the hospital with the aid of his Zimmer frame. I had never dared ask him whether he ever felt, even for a tiny second, that overwhelming feeling of perfection.

I did once gather up enough courage to ask Gyuri Sándor. We happened to be on our way to visit my father after the first operation, as he was recovering in some hospital. We'd arranged to meet in Moszkva Square because it was convenient for him on his way back from work, Gyuri being one of those people who prefers to work till the day he dies. We stood by the flower statue and gazed at the various commercial goings-on: the loud youths, the gypsy traders in their long skirts avoiding the police, the idle day labourers waiting to be picked up for some chore in the city's affluent outskirts. We were like two survivors of an earlier age, turning our heads around like frightened chickens.

'Gyuri, my dear, have you ever been in love?' I asked, slightly to my own surprise.

When in his late forties, Gyuri had married one of his colleagues at work, a woman who, like him, was the only survivor of a once-thriving Jewish family. Fugitive with fugitive, stray seed with stray seed. Marriage then was often a covenant between survivors, a form of defence and defiance. They had no children. Gyuri studied our children with the curiosity of an anthropologist. He died just as my children were getting to the age when they could have started having proper conversations.

Gyuri stood next to me, wearing a tie and an impeccably

tailored suit, his face expressionless, as if he hadn't heard my question.

'What's your problem?' His clever eyes flashed at me behind his glasses. Because of the fierce light I couldn't tell whether he was smiling or just screwing up his eyes against the sun.

'I asked if you have ever been truly happy in love,' I persisted. 'If there was a moment in your life when you said: This is it; time should stop right here.'

Gyuri gazed at the queue of people at the ticket office, lost in thought. Then he gave me a cheeky grin.

'Ah yes. Talking about Faust reminds me to thank you for the Camões book. An excellent translation. It's an essential work. You really should read it.'

I sighed and gave up, and took his arm as we set off slowly for the 56 tram.

A couple of years later, shortly after waking one morning, Gyuri had a stroke. He lay slumped at the foot of the bed, looking helplessly at his wife who was having coffee in the armchair. The woman, who returned from deportation unharmed but had lost a leg in 1956, did not see anything wrong with him, hobbled out to fetch the newspaper and threw it into his lap. Gyuri sat there with the copy of *Népszabadság* in his lap, watching astonished as the world unwound in slow motion, until the haemorrhage in his brain started to make him feel sick. By the time they rang my mother, it was too late. Gyuri took two weeks to die. My father and I visited him in hospital every day.

'Gyuri, my dear, do you want to live?' I bent over him to say once while my father nipped out on some errand.

Without his glasses his face looked naked. He blinked at me through his left eye and a teardrop started meandering down the wrinkles of his face, as though seeking a path. His wife, a sharp-witted, grim-humoured commissar of a creature, died a couple of months after him. When their flat had to be emptied, my mother spent days clearing the pantry of flour, sugar and bottles of sunflower oil long past their use-by date.

It was in Mexico that I met the second great love of my life. I had arrived there with the modest mission to liberate the Latin American continent. My father, my sister and I had divided the world between us: he watched over Eastern Europe, my sister took care of Africa and I, out of my great enthusiasm for Che Guevara and the heroes of the Spanish Civil War, took on Latin America. I had learned Spanish and read everything I could get hold of back home to prepare myself for the task, and, after one or two unsuccessful attempts, won a scholarship that took me to my mission field. I had no idea that this innocent-looking research trip would completely change my life. It's true that I had had a few encounters with sobering reality before, but every time I returned home my father saw to it that any resulting cracks in the façade should be quickly plastered over. This time I was far away in Mexico and the cracking process became irreversible. To nobody's surprise, I did not succeed in liberating Latin America. It became apparent pretty quickly that I was again the victim of a gross semantic misunderstanding. It was Latin America that liberated me.

My father read thick books in English and in German, but when he read aloud it was impossible to understand him because he spoke phonetically, as political prisoners did in the past, learning the languages of people they could never visit. On his rare ventures to the West, my father stumbled haplessly along the tangled paths of a living language. Fortunately there was always some printed matter he could use as a butterfly net to catch the odd bit of speech as it fluttered past him so that he could study it at his leisure. He generally managed in this way. Perhaps my father saw the truth, as presented to his eyes behind the Iron Curtain, over-literally, too. He had no problems of interpretation in the East, not only because of his perfect knowledge of Russian and Czech and the linguistic gift he inherited from his father that enabled him to understand practically everything, but because reality seemed to adjust itself to the twisted and simplified language that was applied to it.

Western languages were pure fiction to me, too, and for a long time I didn't see the point of wasting my time on them. I learnt English after university, through miscellaneous courses, having discovered that I couldn't get by without it. When, a couple of years later, I was awarded a scholarship to England, I was happily making my way home with the good news, thinking about how once there in foggy Albion I could drop into an ordinary English shop and ask for a bottle of milk in Shakespeare's language, and I grinned so widely that a man passing me in the street stopped and raised his eyebrow expectantly. I could of course ask for milk in Pushkin's language as well, during my student exchange trips to the Soviet Union, but this did not always lead to the desired results. Spanish was a completely different matter, because it was the language of my mission; but I also felt from the start that it was the language of the heart.

My first trip to the West had led me to the south, to a Spain slowly recovering after the death of Franco, where decades of lies, silence, forbidden history and unremitting oppression had left terrible scars that had not yet healed. All this felt familiar. I also started to recognise the forms of resistance to oppression. Since my travel companions with whom I had set out on the Great Adventure could not resist the lures of jeans, hot-dogs and porn and got stuck at the very first Western place where we had to change trains – in the preternaturally clean city of Zurich – I had to continue my discovery of the Western world all alone. And, just as on my unforgettable Polish journey, it was as if an invisible companion were leading me by the hand.

It was the first time in my life that I had used a Western language in its country of origin. I was delighted to note that here words revealed realities rather than hid them. One night, in a suburb of Seville, I listened breathlessly to a series of flamenco musicians performing on a make-do stage and decided that everything Lorca had to say on the nature of the *duende* was true. In Córdoba I bowed before the statue of the turbaned Maimonides on the fringe of the Judería district, and cursed in Hungarian when I saw that they had built a Catholic cathedral in the middle of the Great Mosque, as if they had ruined one of my personal treasures. I spent hours sitting under the starry vault of the Alhambra in Granada, dreaming of the vanished Muslim,

Jewish, Christian and pagan worlds that had conjured this extraordinary beauty into existence.

When I managed to tear myself away from this 'paradise on Earth', I descended to the city and spent the afternoon listening to striking workers from the tile factory as they discussed matters in a smoke-filled office. Suddenly one of them turned to me and asked me what I, a living beneficiary of really-existing socialism, thought about the problem they wanted to elucidate. On a sheet torn from my exercise book with sweaty hands I made a sketch of Marx's theory of exploitation, silently thanking the heavens that my mind hadn't been completely befuddled by Parmenides at that study camp on *Das Kapital* so many years ago. Everything I had learned back home and was becoming ever less relevant under the conditions of a reality that had been losing connection with its proclaimed values unexpectedly made sense here. One morning in Barcelona, as I leant out of the window for a breath of fresh air after a night of conversation, I saw the multicoloured ceramic giraffes of the Sagrada Familia emerge out of the dawn mist. Reality was far more fascinating then anything I had ever imagined before. 'It's OK, it's all right,' Great Uncle Reality muttered. 'You can close your mouth now.'

I took my next lesson in reality two years later, on my first hard-won Western student exchange trip. After the Big Discoveries, now the lesson was to learn how to make distinctions. I found myself in Galicia, in the westernmost part of Spain, on the periphery of the European periphery, sitting with Rodolfo, an uneducated joiner and anarchist who had grown up in orphanages meant for the children of murdered Republicans and who had spent the bulk of his youth in Franco's prisons. In the evenings a group of his friends – teachers, doctors, artists and manual workers – would meet in his flat; we made the round of local bars and cafés, vehemently discussing life's great questions with a lot of laughter and flowery words, before returning to Rodolfo's flat, where talk would go on for ever.

I listened attentively to their stories. I listened as they told me how, ever since the death of Trotsky, the cause of freedom was fatally divided because poor Leon had dared to suggest that the final struggle had not yet been won, that the revolution fought to make life more human had given birth to a terrible monster. Which was why Stalin had sent a man with an ice-pick after him to picturesque Coyoacán in Mexico, where I was to settle a few years later, and this is what lay behind Comrade Semprún's strayings into the swamps of Eurocommunism, too. Now I understood that not even the Spanish Civil War had been a struggle between Good and Evil; that it wasn't just a question of Them shooting at Us, but that We had been shooting at ourselves, and that that was why the outcome was even more catastrophic than I had previously imagined. I understood now how all those handsome, bearded young men with burning eyes who emerged from the forests of Latin America tended to become unbridled killers or silent accomplices to killing, much as their Eastern European predecessors with their open white shirts had done once, except if they remained miraculously bound by an obstinate respect for truth, always providing they hadn't been eliminated by their comrades first.

By now I had accepted the truth that the heroic Soviet army of liberation really had raped girls and young women, and that they really had stopped outside Warsaw so as to allow the Germans to burn down what remained of the city, and that that took place after they really had massacred leading Polish officers in Katyń forest, precisely as my Polish friends had claimed years before on that memorable journey to Poland. I had understood that the Bund, the republicans, the socialists, the social democrats and the moderate democrats, everyone, in fact, who had dared stand up to the twin forces of totalitarianism which had been attacking them from both sides since the 1930s was condemned to death; that, if nothing else, one had to believe the account of Marguerite Buber-Neumann and acknowledge that those who survived Hitler's death camps often found themselves in the Gulag, and vice versa; that oppression and spiritual impoverishment ran through families, workplaces, schools and all intimate relations, and that we had to fight them with all means at our disposal if we wanted to live in a dignified, human way.

When Rodolfo saw that the lesson was getting me down a little, he rose and started searching his bookshelves. Lack of education did not prevent him from being a passionate reader. Instead of smelling salts he gave me a book by Arthur Koestler.

'See, this guy was from your neck of the woods. He understood what happened here.'

'Mmm,' I mumbled. 'Koestler, a fine Hungarian name.'

It was the Hispanic world that was fated to arrange my most dramatic encounters with reality. It was as if it was there that I had to receive my invisible heritage from my unknown ancestors. Only years later did I discover from Gigi that our family's first exile was from Spain, and that our ancestors were forced to leave the very same summer that the first ships left Andalusia for a new Garden of Eden that they called New Spain, then later Mexico.

Mexico was where I finally made top grade in reality studies. It was such a peculiar mixture of the exotic and the familiar that all I had to get used to were the altitude sickness and the regular earthquakes, along with all the images of poverty that I had not previously encountered back home in Hungary. Concerning the latter, I concluded that much of what I had considered perfectly natural at home was in fact the product of social struggle; that the change in political system that had rescued my mother, and millions like her, from misery had not yet occurred in this spellbinding country and that for much of the world the hunger for bread was still more urgent than the hunger for knowledge.

Arriving in the New World, I was surprised to find all my senses awakened. Everything I had previously known suddenly appeared in a new light. Meandering down the zigzag streets of Coyoacán I was no longer bound by the thousand strands that had tied me to the past. The words offered to veil the ever-less-comfortable reality back home (like talk about really-existing socialism instead of socialism) were missing here; I could call everything by its true name. The centuries of ruthless oppression, successive revolutions betrayed and reversed, the shadow of the Big Neighbour, the series of territorial losses, the institutionalised Party of the Revolution kept in power for decades through various combinations of corruption, repression and paternalism – all these were extremely familiar. One day I woke thinking that the laws that bound our lives back home, that I had always taken to be natural, lacked all meaning. Or rather, their sole meaning was to keep us under control, because freedom was an ungovernable danger. 'Dear Fülöp,' I wrote to my father in a rare but spirited letter. 'We're so scared of everything at home we don't even know what life is.'

One afternoon I was at the zoo in Villahermosa when, looking at the tiger skin and noting the windings of the snakes, I recognised the classic patterns engraved on stone, in gold or obsidian in great masterpieces. I had spent years in the reading room of the Ernő Szabó central library, leafing through albums of reproductions of which these were the originals. I had been driven by such a desire to encounter reality in all its brilliance that I would often push aside my sheets of paper and leave my university office to take long train journeys and bumpy bus rides through the immense country, over hills, down valleys, through dense forests, my eyes wide open, wanting to register every face, every scene, every object they came across. It was there, at the end of one of these trips, on the Yucatán isthmus, where the long-destroyed palaces of ancient people lay in ruins overgrown by tropical vegetation, that I met the man who was to send me the letter in the blue envelope.

Lost in thought, I gazed at the small round letters that

once meant life to me. At that time, which seems an infinity ago now, we both felt a new sense of hope. We were survivors of two decimated tribes condemned to death and the bare fact that we found ourselves in each other's arms seemed to prove that it was possible to make a new beginning.

The letters slalomed over invisible blue hills of paper, bright beads strung on an invisible lace of love, anxiety and desire. Even handwriting, that mirror of the soul, is slowly dying, I thought, like all those varieties of corn or those turtles that laid their eggs on the seashore, swept away by the barbarism of technologies unable to respect minute differences. We might be the last generation to appreciate the hard-won elegance of writing, the smoothness of paper, the sense of a pen or pencil sliding over a limitless incline, the loops that capture an entire life, the struggle with intangible matters whereby a nothing becomes a word. Who, in an evanescent age of cheap telephones, email and texting will still be willing to commit their thoughts to paper and send those thoughts to some other person? The new generations growing up with computers and video clips, who even do their homework on machines: will they learn to write, will they produce such everyday, unconscious reflections of their soul? Will there be souls at all?

I hated the thought of returning from Mexico. All the reasons for returning – my vocation, my boyfriend waiting for me, the call of the mother country and the hope of repairing really-existing socialism from the inside – seemed poor recompense for the enormous loss against which I was preparing myself. When I could no longer postpone the journey and all the details were fixed, I set out for the prosperous quarter of Mexico City where the office dealing with my official business was situated. Before stepping into the glass palace, I had to stop for a minute in the constant chaos of blaring horns, the exhaust fumes of buses, the bellowing of street vendors, the beggar child at the red light nipping to car windows, bored young rich men in their air-conditioned vehicles, pretty fake blondes lipsticked and pouting, policemen in gloves whistling and waving their arms, great towering office blocks, swaying palm trees, and blinding advertisements. Something odd happened. I turned up the collar of my linen jacket and pressed my hands into my pockets. I was cold.

In the unusual cold of that autumn morning, I was suddenly transported to the forgotten mornings of childhood, when I first had to wear a coat on my way to school; when, still sleepy and shivering, I walked through the doorway into the low sun of Németvölgyi Road, where I could see my breath rising before me. There were hardly any cars in the street at that time; it was the pattering footsteps of pedestrians and the loud chorus of birds that escorted me as I made my way slowly, almost floating in the light. There was always a chestnut that happened to drop to the broken pavement before me. I'd pick it up, wipe the white ash from it and squeeze it in my palm. Ten thousand four hundred kilometres away, in the deafening cacophony of the Lomas de Chapultepec in Mexico City, before I even had the ticket for the flight in my hands, my body had already returned through the morning chill. You're a traitor to the cause, I whispered to myself, and quickly stepped through the automatic doors.

As I had suspected, my return to Hungary had catastrophic consequences. The invisible chains that had previously dragged me home had snapped one by one, like worn-out guitar strings. Their last sorry reverberations kept echoing in my head. Twang, twang, twang. It looked like the only reason for coming home was that all such strings should finally be broken and that I should drop into the empty space without any safety net. The expanded dimensions of my being couldn't be squeezed back into the narrow confines of normality. Every effort to do so was excruciatingly painful. My parents couldn't understand what was happening to me and watched my struggles with growing concern. My friends stood around, sympathetic but helpless. My boyfriend left me. I went to work each morning, properly programmed, but once I was home at the end of the day I remembered nothing of what I had done. Nor did I make any attempt to remember things. It was autumn and there in autumn's shadows lurked, as Vörösmarty put it, 'winter and silence and snow and death'.

A couple of weeks after my return, I was no longer a member of the advance guard.

> What we nurtured is quite gone,
> It's what the enemy's now protecting.
> I drop the imaginary gun
> I spent thirty years perfecting.

I recited Attila József's lines, my face aglow, to the astonished Party secretary (a good-hearted old lady) as I handed back the red Party membership book that entitled me to improve really-existing socialism from within. My father wasn't interested in my recitation. He retired into his shell to mourn me, his lost child. I was surprised to see how upset he was because I thought he had long given up on me. Years before, when I first found myself in waters the appropriate authorities declared out of bounds, my father tried to convince me of the dangers of such folly by reasoning with me, before losing his temper and declaring that I was no longer his daughter. I had not the least intention of breaking with my parents, but after this I thought it best to avoid our regular Sunday lunches. My mother took to her bed and, a couple of weeks later, my father rang me to suggest we should talk things over. We walked for hours in the Castle district, the result of which was that my father no longer tried to convert me to the true path and I returned to the family table. Not much later I left the country with a legal passport and official permission. The next time we talked politics was when the first Yugoslav war broke out.

ꝏ

My dear sister,
Spring doesn't want to arrive. We had a day of sunshine then we spent three days shivering. The animals are confused, too. I counted the nests by the lake this morning: there are seven, but three of them are so badly placed that they'll get swept away by the first storm. I went for my walk, greeted the three-hundred-year-old cedar of Lebanon and, on my way home, by the small

bay, I saw a swan sitting on three enormous greenish eggs. I had already spotted a young man in the distance standing very still and watching the nest. When I reached him I glanced at his face; he looked so desperate I almost touched him on the elbow. But I didn't. I withdrew my hand and hurried home in a bad mood. I am teaching the children the old 'Ballad of Borbála Angoli' as well as Attila József and János Arany, and reading them the *Book of Kings*. I drag them to the Kunsthistorische Museum so they may experience Rembrandt and feel at home in this world. But then I feel terrified that by the time they grow up all those things that I regard as the cornerstones of my own being will have become meaningless; that I am filling their heads with all kinds of useless stuff, the way our father filled ours. What grounds do we have for claiming we are different sorts of parents?

Love

Y

☙

Dear Miki,

The reason I didn't like the Rabbi's speech at Kol Nidre is because I believe that the synagogue is not the place for political agitation: neither synagogue nor church should instruct us how to vote. It might be that my sense of being an outsider makes me vain and over-sensitive but, for me, the dream of a pure Jewish state is as unacceptable as a pure Hungarian state, as Greater Serbia for the Serbs and the rest. Of course I know there are the historical circumstances, but even so I reject it. There are always 'historical circumstances'. The existence of Israel matters to me, too, but if we lived there I am sure we would look at it in the same tortured, critical way as, say, David Grossman or Amos Oz do. At least I hope that the struggle for survival would not altogether distort our values.

I should also say that I have no problem at all with the fact that the majority of Jews live outside Israel. That's good for both parties. We can learn from each other. How else could we represent the values that we were, if my memory serves me right, chosen to represent? What would Kafka have written, or Celan, or Canetti, had they not been born in completely multi-ethnic Prague, Czernowitz and Ruse?

Love

Y

☙

In the winter following my father's death, my mother got on a plane with us and we flew to California to visit Steven's family and friends. We left my father at home in the frozen ground of the Németvölgyi Road cemetery while we buckled up our safety belts in the spirit of adventure. My mother, whom it had taken us a long time to persuade to travel, was like a little girl discovering the big wide world. It made life easier that all this happened before Bush Junior's second presidency and 9/11; the proud empire of the no-longer bipolar world was not constantly rubbing it in where the power lay. When my mother saw that the mighty bastion of imperialism was also populated by human beings, she packed away her prejudices and resolved to take it all in. She reined in her much-noted sensibilities and made such extraordinary observations that I never ceased to be astonished. From this point of view it helped that it was the first time in her life she had travelled to an entirely new place without my father, whose judgements had always been very important to her. We hardly mentioned his absence;

the environment was so different. What was more, we had given winter the runaround. Even on New Year's Day my mother was more concerned about rescuing my children's caps from the sea breeze than with the fact it was the first New Year she had seen in without my father.

When she returned to Budapest a couple of weeks later, I felt we had navigated the first circle of mourning remarkably well. It seemed that even my father was happy to convey his sense of satisfaction. Two days after my mother's return home, the ancient East German food processor that was of considerable importance to her ever-more-baroque ventures into cookery finally gave up the ghost. My mother did the rounds of the city's household supply shops, but they just laughed at her. East Germany? What on Earth is this, madam? And the French manufacturer Moulinex has just gone bankrupt! Maybe in the spring, madam, if we're lucky. It seemed that chopping was out of the question for a while. But that was where my father came in. Not long after my mother decided to stop bothering with the shops, my father's study produced a brand new East German mincer.

'Didn't I tell you it might come in useful some time?'

ଓ

Ten days after the first anniversary of my father's death, I found myself, to my own surprise, in the synagogue at Nyíregyháza where those members of my family who had survived to this stage had been taken before deportation. I stood a while in the cold, echoing hall, thinking how terrible the silence in synagogues was. No more prayers, no crowds, no weeping, no squabbling. Only the worn stairs, only the trees seen through the windows remained. Only when I am inside, looking out, are they, the dead, present.

ര

Two summers after my father's death, I had to go on a study trip to the newly dismembered Yugoslavia. I felt such anxiety that the children watched my preparations with concern. Just as two years previously, when I feared my father might drag me down into the dark with him, now I had the entirely illogical feeling that I might become the first sacrificial pawn in his long game of chess with Yugoslavia.

'If you die you'll give me your bracelet, won't you?' my daughter asked me when I tucked myself into bed beside her to wish her goodnight. That was rather too scary for comfort.

According to the calendar, it was spring when I touched down in Pristina, at an airfield that looked more like an unploughed field than a runway, then fought my way through the ring of grim-faced men waiting silently and impatiently at the exit. There was no trace of spring in the fields. It was as if nature had not yet had time to recover from the violence of two years before. The evidence of war was apparent everywhere: on bitter faces, in smashed windowpanes, on ripped-up pavements and walls blackened by smoke. Despite the order established, with great difficulty, by international forces, the embers of violence were still glowing. Late at night, alone in the bullet-riddled hotel towering over the town, whose upper floors were in a state of utter disrepair, I listened to the noises of the night in case I could catch the 'sweet silence' Ivo Andrić once wrote about. But the icy wind whistling through the window brought only shouts, the drumming of feet and the unsettling sound of speeding cars. There was no crackle of gunfire, only the threat of it at any moment.

The dawn before we left Kosovo, the minibus of some British organisation rolled up at the hotel entrance because there were no taxis, or at least none willing to carry passengers to the border. My colleagues sat me next to the driver, the rest squeezed in the back with the luggage. I did what my father would have done and started asking questions. The young driver had been a schoolteacher who had been sacked soon after Milošević had taken office and who had later continued teaching in the parallel educational network that tried to operate in private flats. Along with other family survivors of the massacre in Kosovo, he had made his way on foot to the Albanian border.

'Look, this is me.' He fished in his back pocket.

I watched frightened as the bus juddered over potholes, but didn't have the nerve to ask him to hang on to the wheel if he didn't mind. The carefully folded German-language newspaper he produced from his wallet showed a Reuters photograph. In it a never-ending queue of people with bundles and suitcases were making their way up a hill top. 'That's me,' said the driver as, by great good fortune, he finally managed to grab the wheel with one hand while using the other to point to a weary-faced young man with what looked like an enormous backpack, his arm around a little girl carrying a doll. I stared in silence at the picture shaking in front of me.

'Do you know who that is on my back?' the man asked. 'That's my cousin. She's paralysed, can't walk. The Serbs snatched her wheelchair so I had to carry her all the way to the border. And do you know why she is paralysed? Because the Serbian doctor wouldn't give her a vaccination.'

I didn't dare ask if there were any other men left in his family that could carry the child. He was the only young man among the group climbing the hill.

'Who is the little girl?' I asked him.

'My daughter, just turned three.' His face brightened into a smile. 'Every time a convoy of Serbians escorted by UN troops passes us, she shouts from the car: "Scum! Fire! Fire!" "Scum" means the Serbs. She keeps shouting "Fire" because every time she sees a uniform it reminds her of our burning house. She doesn't know the difference yet,' he added when he saw I hadn't really understood.

It grew quiet, a quiet disturbed only by the squeaking of the minibus and the bodies being thrown about with the luggage at the back. I cleared my throat.

'And what do you say to her, then?' I asked tentatively.

'Say to who?'

'Your little girl.'

'I try to calm her.'

'But not all Serbs are scum,' I muttered half to myself.

He gave me a quizzical look, then silently turned to face the road again.

'If a child is brought up to hate, there will never be an end to it,' I muttered, still more quietly.

'You saw what we went through,' he retorted.

I noted the wrecked military vehicle at the side of the road, the broken trees, the sacked buildings. My fingers were blenched as I clutched the white plastic handle over the door. I took a deep breath.

'Look, I am a Jew,' I said eventually. I was aware that the noise behind me had stopped. 'Do you know what that means?'

'No,' he answered.

'The People of Israel.'

'Ah,' he said, and thought a little. 'In that case you should know better than anyone,' he almost shouted, turning to me again.

'Absolutely,' I answered. 'I spent decades fearing Germans. But in the end I discovered that it wasn't the Germans I had to fear, but the people who drove them to do such things.'

As far as time and circumstances allowed, I held a rapidly improvised lecture about those who exploited the concept of national identity in oppressive régimes. When we reached the border, he helped me from my seat and quickly turned away. I followed him.

'Goodbye,' I said and extended my hand, aware that I was looking at him rather beseechingly.

He shook my hand as if he didn't want to and went to help unload the luggage, then drove off without looking at me.

Although it was early morning, I felt exhausted and

broken as if I had been breaking stones all day. We walked across the no-man's-land between Kosovo and what was then still the Federal Republic of Yugoslavia, as inconspicuously as we could because at any moment someone might take a shot at us. Once there, we waited for a couple of hours before getting on another minibus. A dour-looking silent man sat next to the driver now. I watched in silence as the trees at the edge of the road rushed by, saw the big Serbian flags planted by the fresh graves and gazed at the tractors puffing at the edges of the road, while to our left glittering Mercedes saloon cars cruised by.

I felt confused walking around Belgrade. I couldn't decide whether the well-dressed, loud young men in the street were protesting for or against the current régime, or whether they were just youths messing about; I couldn't understand why the national flag was displayed from the windows of cars taking people to weddings or why anyone would cover the pedestals of statues with graffiti saying: We love you Slobo, despite the fact that Slobo had spent the last six months in a well-heated cell in The Hague and no one needed to fear him any longer. If there was still killing or if those who had brought it about were still at the peak of their power, this sense of solidarity and collective amnesia might have been explicable. But with Milošević gone, what was the point? Is it true that you become an unwilling accomplice of a crime committed on your behalf?

In all the bitter arguments I had with the inhabitants of the country still known as Yugoslavia, it seemed as if the map drawn up in Karađorđevo between Milošević and the President of Croatia, Franjo Tuđman, showing the dividing up of Bosnia and what it entailed in terms of those hundreds of thousands of people who had been murdered, raped or exiled from their homes, was a secret known to me alone. Everyone I spoke to, from the taxi driver to the ministerial representative, knew only about the havoc caused by NATO's bombings, about the hardship of the NATO embargo, and about Serbian refugees spending the winter freezing in wooden barracks. All this was true but, I insisted, we should start from the speech made by Milošević in 1987 at Kosovo Polje, the speech that led directly to Karađorđevo, the destruction of Bosnia and the cleansing of Kosovo in 1999. There you go again with that same old scrap of paper, they sighed, rolling their eyes. What damage can a scrap of paper do to solid walls and centuries-old bridges, and to flesh-and-blood people?

Only now did I finally understand why my father ranted at me in the hall of the Németvölgyi Road flat claiming that the 'fundamentalist' Izetbegović was set to loose a jihad on the world. It was the peculiar speciality of the Yugoslav war (or any war?) to twist historical facts in order to create a mood of terror. Having read Misha Glenny, Malcolm Noel and other historians of that war, it became clear to me how these deceptions worked, but those affected by them apparently had other sources of information. There was a vast chasm between reality and its representations, but it was pointless me saying that those on the other side were prey to misconceptions and false myths. Misconceptions and false myths formed reality as well. Those people were my own frightening reflection. They were, after all, subject to the same desire for myth and wish-fulfilment as I was, or at least the part of me that was constantly trying to escape the grip of the socialist realist tenant. What was it my mother used to say? 'Being determines consciousness.' Or was it the other way round? When do ideals become false consciousnesses? At what point does the pursuit of myth become murder?

I was relieved to climb the steps to the plane. Up there, riding the highways of the sky, I could admire the crimson light above the layers of cloud and try to imagine what I would tell my father. 'You see what happens when you refuse to face the facts? When you try to sweep the truth, the past, and the sense of responsibility under the carpet?' I muttered to myself grumpily before I remembered he had been dead for years.

☙

My dear friend Miki. Stop. Odysseus is rehabilitated. Stop. He is the archetype of the European soul. Stop. We have learned nothing. Stop. We don't even have the good fortune. Stop. To experience history the second time as farce. Stop. I give up. Stop.Y

☙

My beloved sister,
I was searching the bookshelves this afternoon when, confidently leaning against the Kosztolányi volumes, I spotted Komoróczy's book on Jewish Budapest (an essential work – you really should read it!). I'd long meant to look up what those menorahs were doing on the fence of the hospital on Amerikai Road. I thought

it was bound to be in there. And in fact, I found it in the chapter 'What You Can Still See, but Not in Its Original Form'. The hospital was originally built by the city's Jewish community as the Chevra Kadisa Charity for the Incurable and became a sanatorium after 1919. In the entrance hall, where we sat with our father on our last visit, the walls are so bare because the marble memorial tablets commemorating the builders and funders were turned facing into the wall at the time of the 1985 renovation.

The three Jewish hospital foundations, as conceived by Béla Lajta, were to resemble the lay-outs of village synagogues, with buildings around a yard. They were surrounded by a huge garden that extended as far as Korong Street, the street where we'd go for coffee sometimes. A few houses beyond the pastry shop in the single-storey building was Attila József's last flat. At the end of the street was the Institute for the Blind. Next to the entrance, on the right, you can still see the metal notice in Braille with the first words of Vörösmarty's 'Appeal', so the little blind Jewish children should never forget: 'To your country be forever true.'

Do you think our father knew this?

Love

Y

P.S. Today, on the way home from the park with the kids, we saw a swan that had built its nest on top of a pile of rubbish, next to a gutter. It was a pretty nest made of dead leaves, broken twigs and bits of plastic bottles and the swan was struggling with a bigger piece of branch that kept slipping out of its beak. It wouldn't give up, and time and time again it tried, despite everything, to establish it as a part of its home. I was very impressed to see how much strength that relatively small body possessed and started to drift off pondering about eternal struggle when I realised that we were late and had to run. Hats off to the swans!

❧

My father was stirring Barbon shaving foam in the bathroom, humming to himself. I sat on the small stool watching as his face disappeared under the foam so that the skin might reappear fresh and flushed in the stripes following the careful strokes of his razor. His skin made a barely audible scraping noise. Occasionally he cut himself and small red patches spread across his face. My father seemed enormous, viewed from that small stool, but as the years went by he shrank. Once I was grown-up and somewhat taller, I sometimes stopped leaning against the bathroom door and hardly needed to raise my head to view the morning ritual. My father was humming the letter aria '*E lucevan le stelle*' from *Tosca*. I knew from family legend that *Tosca* was my grandfather Lajos's favourite opera and that he particularly liked the letter aria, in which the hero, in full throat, declares: 'Why should I die when I want to live? I want to live!' – or something like that. My father did not sing in full throat because his mouth was closed on account of the shaving foam, but when he got to this part the humming definitely grew louder.

My father had long stopped humming while he shaved and I myself was a long way from the bathroom in Németvölgyi Road the next time I heard the melody. A couple of days after Simon's birth, when I made my first tentative foray down to the hospital yard, I heard it pouring through an open window. I stood under the window with my eyes closed as if I was sunbathing, letting the music flow over me. But I couldn't quite bring myself to go to the opera. When we were young, my sister and I were subjected to opera – all in the memory of my grandfather, of course – to such an extent that we both grew to regard it as a form of torture. Although torture turned to comedy when our parents took us to see a visiting Soviet company perform *Eugene Onegin*. Two clumsy mountains of flesh were pining for love of each other. The leading man might have had a fine voice, but his mouth was crooked. We were bursting with suppressed laughter and when, in one unguarded moment, we glanced at each other, we did indeed burst out laughing. We were immediately dismissed from the sanctuary of the opera house. Unshaken by this terrible punishment, we played at opera for years, choking and giggling in bed after lights out. 'Here's your cloak, Eugene Crookmouth,' I piped, with melodramatic gestures. And at the finale I always burst out: 'Though I die of grief, I will never be yours, Crookmouth Onegiiiiin!' Then we swapped and my sister played Tatiana.

On what would have been my father's seventy-fifth birthday and close to the third anniversary of his death, I found myself sitting in the Grand Théâtre in Geneva awaiting the letter aria. That weekend Geneva had its Festival of Music, when the whole town becomes a series of concert halls: there is music everywhere and people move happily around from one performance to another. In the afternoon the children and I were wandering around when, passing by the Grand Théâtre, I saw that the opera season was closing with *Tosca*. On the spur of the moment, we went into the cool entrance hall and waited in the long queue for unreserved tickets. I got one of the last. We dashed home, I ran the children a bath, shared out the various treasures gathered that day and, quickly splashing some water over my own body, grabbed the first decent outfit I could find in my wardrobe and flew down the stairs.

'I'm off to meet Grandfather!' I shouted to the children, who were busy figuring out what the lipstick stains on their cheeks reminded them of.

When I sank into the extra chair on the first tier of the balcony, all I could think of for a while was getting my breath back and wondering if everything was all right at home. Only slowly did the music manage to exert its spell on me. I sat there, on my dead father's birthday, with dead Gigi's watch on my wrist, in a silk dress chosen by another dead woman, my lungs working hard, the sweat running down my back, a whole day's worth of dust on my naked feet, every nerve alive. To my greatest surprise, it was not my father that emerged from the music but my grandfather, Lajos. When, in the first major duet, Cavaradossi, the painter, is courting his beloved, the beautiful, famous singer Tosca, suddenly I felt quite sure that my grandfather would have hummed the same tune, in exactly the same way, to my grandmother, his cheek to her cheek, murmuring how there was nothing brighter than her brilliant dark eyes. Since I had no previous idea what happened in the opera, except in the letter aria, it wasn't just the music but the story that carried me away. To my amazement, I discovered political drama under the romance. The values of liberty, love, solidarity and enlightenment were all embodied in the music along with the struggle against the powers of darkness, the very ideas my dead grandfather passed on to my father, the ideas with which I too had been brought up, though by that time the brew had been spiced up with a few ingredients of communism.

In the story, Cavaradossi promises the consul of the fallen Roman republic that he will save him though it will cost him his life, because the cause of freedom is what matters most to both of them. When, at the end of the opera, he is preparing to die, the knowledge that he has remained true to his ideals gives him strength. To what ideals could my grandfather remain true? What faith, what love, what values persisted in him? Did he think of the letter aria when they took him away to kill him? Did he recall the soaring melody, and could it out-soar the whistling of the icy wind, the groaning of his fellow prisoners and the rattle of gunfire after which there could only be eternal silence? Immersed in that flood of music, I saw my grandfather Lajos for the first time, or, more accurately, I saw what he saw: the bare branches of winter trees, those great dark admonitory bones against the leaden sky, the clouds suddenly rising above the earth; I saw the earth sliding away, the bushes shrouded in despair, the dark pools rising to my eyes. 'Is all this happening to me?' he may have asked himself, as my father may have asked himself, too, that evening when my mother told him that his cancer was back, just as I sometimes asked myself. 'Is this really happening to me?' Grandfather Lajos might have asked as he finally hit the dried mud of the ground under his feet.

CR

The fourth summer after my father died, I was on my way to town one afternoon, on the same line I had taken all those times my father was in hospital. I was in a sticky, foul mood. Maybe life is indeed no more than a meaningless measuring exercise between two arbitrarily drawn lines, beyond which lies nothing but indifferent matter, and between which there is only violence, stupidity and egotism. It may be that life really is a tale told by an idiot, full of sound and fury signifying nothing. The paper lay open in my lap but I didn't feel like reading it. I was staring at the plastic seating and waiting for the train to start. When the doors closed, I looked up. At the end of the carriage there stood a couple, an Asian girl and a Hungarian boy, clinched in an embrace. They bent towards each other drawn by the shy attraction of first love. They exchanged a word now and then, in Hungarian as far as I could tell in the noise, and gave a light laugh, like a soft breeze ruffling the surface of a lake.

A group of boys in heavy boots got on at Batthány Square. A couple of times they drew themselves up on the aluminium handles above their heads and shouted loudly to each other, happily slapping each other's shaved heads. Once they had established their territory in the middle of the coach, they ran half-closed eyes over the rest of it. Their eyes fixed on the young couple. As if on cue, they started singing a song the meaning of which, as far as I could tell, was that foreigners should go home and no longer sully the sacred soil of our country. In the refrain I could make out the repeated phrase 'slitty-eyed', aimed at the lovers. That I heard clearly enough because we were approaching a station. Suddenly I was overcome by indignation and fear. My fellow passengers were busily staring at the non-existent view or burying their heads in their papers. The few eyes that dared follow events showed the same mixture of terror and anger as mine probably did. I resolved to say something once the train reached Deák Square, but here both the couple and the gang got off. As the couple moved to the door I could see they were no longer radiantly happy, that they hung their heads and clutched each other's hands anxiously as they stepped from the swaying coach, giving the boot boys plenty of room before ascending the moving stairs.

I hurried out of the subway as if on urgent business and walked rapidly towards the Danube. I saw the long queues of cars, the pedestrians as they shoved each other impatiently out of the way, as if they had been cut off from their life supply on the way from their computer screen to their TV screen, or the other way round. I saw tempers flare and tasted the poison pouring from their mouths; I heard the inane chatter that constantly rolls through the street with them. I stood on the embankment and gazed at the city, out of sorts with itself as the ashen twilight slowly covered it. The old rat, the ancient rat that Attila József saw in the 1930s, that 'ancient rat that spreads disease among us: unconsidered, un-thought-out thought', had been chewing away at us, but how big had it grown in the meantime; good God, how enormous it was.

ଔ

It was on a morning walk, several years after my father died, that it first occurred to me that I should really thank him for keeping quiet about the past. It might not have been a simple question of self-denial, he might just have wanted to save us from whatever was breaking his own back. Perhaps it wasn't only the terror he couldn't speak about, but the shame, too, the shame of all he was obliged to witness and yet carry on living. What options do survivors have once they have escaped? Should they bury the past for ever, or remain victims for ever? Should they vow 'to forgive but not forget', or should they take revenge? Should they become ever-vigilant guardians of memory, like Elie Wiesel, or chroniclers of the nameless millions of victims of colonialism, like André Schwarz-Bart? Should they become silent, like Marek Edelman, who was reluctant to say anything for decades after the ghetto uprising, and only talked about his heart patients in the Sterling hospital of Łódź ?

Often even the families of those returning from the camps were incapable of hearing their stories through – that is, even if the victims were able to tell them, which was rarely the case. The experience became incommunicable. Primo Levi, Tadeusz Borowski, Paul Celan had all wanted to tell what had happened to them so such things should never happen again, but they soon understood that it was better to keep quiet. The silence destroyed them in due course. It was only the fortunate few who were afforded the opportunity, decades later, once time had inevitably swept away the greater part of the terrible remembered past, of speaking about what had happened. The trauma of survival became unresolvable for lack of catharsis. Normal everyday life could comprehend neither the existence of hell, nor the extraordinary ordeal of escaping it. The world no longer made sense.

Returning from the Gulag must have been even more soul-destroying. Once he was liberated, the nightmare continued for the Russian writer Varlam Shalamov, but the reflex of survival had so soaked into him that he no longer felt entitled even to kill himself. He perished, deaf and blind, in a mental institute and it was years before anyone paid attention to his words. When the main character in Vasily Grossman's *Everything Flows*, Ivan Grigoryevich, returns from the camps after many years, all he says is that prison outside has slightly bigger cells, but he still has to fight each day for his bowl of thin soup.

The burden of silence I inherited from my father might have been easier to bear than confronting the facts. Perhaps I should in fact be grateful to him, as he angrily pointed out to me once. His past did not burden my childhood, or at least not on a conscious level, and I, unlike him, grew up in innocence and, by the time I lost that innocence, I was capable of coping with that loss. It might be thanks to that innocent childhood that, unlike a good many children of survivors, I have never been tempted to leap through the window when seized by overwhelming happiness. I have wanted to enjoy every moment of happiness, because I know it will come to an end sooner or later.

And because my parents brought me up not with a past that could never be spoken about, but with the promise of a bright human future, however unfulfilled in their lifetime, or even in mine, I retain the memory of those brilliant historical moments when humanity was at its best, when it showed me the face I wished to see as its true face, even if those moments were unforgivably rare, and even if they often took place in circumstances that testified to the murderous egotism of the human soul. Even in the histories of the camps, I clung to moments at which, say, Ana Novac leans from the window of her barrack in Auschwitz to offer water to those condemned to death; when the Czech writer Milena Jesenská, even on her deathbed, plans a party for her fellow prisoners; when Resnik, the Polish prisoner, helps Primo Levi carry the heavy beam, and when the hero of Kertész's *Kaddish* is lying on a stretcher on his way to the camp hospital and the Teacher runs after him to give him his daily ration.

☙

My father took on ever-more volatile forms after his death. His real being dissolved behind ever-neater stories. Our living images of him were unconsciously displaced by photographs, and even though we occasionally discovered a set of as-yet-unread notes in the now manageable anarchy of his deserted study, they no longer upset us as much as they had done in the first few months. Mourning became an experience we could share, like first love, like a new idea, or the discovery of a good book. Every time someone close to me lost a friend or relative, I got better at consoling them. Our visits to the cemetery became part of long walks; the choice of flowers slowly became more important than those tiny rituals by which the children could conjure my father back to life. There was still the bitter taste of coffee in the morning, a street corner or two that made my heart ache each time I visited home: here once, here no longer, never again. My father returned most often in dreams, most often to my mother. In them they were generally starting on a journey and my mother was happy to let him guide her through unknown worlds. Waking was always agony. However my mother tried to drown her grief in feverish bouts of cooking, I would wake in the mornings with the sense of deep mourning hanging about the flat, like an enormous, dark-winged bird.

I saw him for the last time one summer three years after his death, after a conference in Barcelona as I was rushing from the metro station to my hotel to pick up a suitcase I had left behind because, of course, I had stretched time to the last minute. An ageing couple were walking towards me on the pavement. As I ran past them, a familiar face looked up at me for a second with the inward, almost absent look my father wore at the end. A few paces on, when the connection between the image and its possible location came to me, I stopped but dared not turn round. I don't know if I was afraid that it would be a completely different face or that I would miss the flight if I didn't make the next airport bus, but it was only when I was on the bus, when I leaned back in my seat exhausted, that it occurred to me that it was here he had brought my mother as a birthday present the year before he died and that it was in this city that I myself had first breathed the dizzying air of freedom. It was here that he walked the streets on the last journey of his life, with the same childish sense of wonder he felt every time he left home; perhaps it was here, in an unfamiliar city, that he bequeathed his features to a stranger, so that I should find him years after his death and briefly greet him again.

One night Simon dreamt that he had gone out by himself to visit my father in the cemetery. The moment that he placed the stone on the grave, it was bathed in light, the flowers came to life and a dark shadow emerged from the earth. He took the stone that was emitting a pale light as though it were a lantern and set off home through the silent city. Simon followed him, his heart pounding with excitement. Everyone was asleep in the flat in Németvölgyi Road. When they arrived, my father sat down at his accustomed place at the desk and leaned over a sheet of white paper on which someone had already started drawing the first letter of the alphabet.

Acknowledgements

Thanks to my family, friends and acquaintances whose lives and histories, in various ways, were woven into this book. Special thanks to George Klein, Imre Kertész, Magda van der Ende, Anikó Vári, Mariann Kiss, György Turán and a nameless swan, without whom this book would have never been published.

Author's Note

Unlike geographical Hungary (93,030 square kilometres, 10 million inhabitants), Hungarian literature is a vast, extremely rich country that is unfortunately mostly inaccessible to non-Hungarian speakers. There are, however, some excellent translations available in English, thanks to a few committed and gifted translators.

Most of the poems quoted in the text can be found in the following anthologies:

In Quest of the 'Miracle Stag': The Poetry of Hungary: An Anthology of Hungarian Poetry in English Translation from the 13th Century to the Present, edited by Ádám Makkai (Chicago: Atlantis-Centaur, 1996; second revised edition, Budapest: Tertia; Chicago: Atlantis-Centaur: Framo Publishing, 2000).

The Colonnade of Teeth: Modern Hungarian Poetry, edited by George Gömöri and George Szirtes (Newcastle-upon-Tyne: Bloodaxe Books, 1996).

The Lost Rider: A Bilingual Anthology, selected and edited by Péter Dávidházi, Győző Ferenc, László Kúnos, Szabolcs Várady and George Szirtes (Budapest: Corvina Books Ltd, second edition, 1999).

There is also a bibliography of translated poems by Christina Peter: 'An Annotated Bibliography of Hungarian Poetry in English

Translation' in *The Audit is Done, European Cultural Review* no. 14, 2004: http://www.c3.hu/~eufuzetek/en/eng/14/index.php.

Quotes:

p. 43. Sándor Petőfi, *Egész úton hazafelé* ('On My Way Home'), translated by George Szirtes.

p. 91. Miklós Radnóti, *Ikrek hava* ('Under Gemini'), translated by Kenneth McRobbie; *Razglednicák*, translated by Zsuzsanna Ozsváth and Frederick Turner.

p. 94. Attila József, *Reménytelenül* ('Without Hope'), translated by George Szirtes.

p. 141. Sándor Petőfi, *Szabadság, szerelem* ('Freedom, Love'), translated by Anton Nyerges.

p. 147. Árpád Farkas, *Mikor az öregemberek mosakodnak* ('When Old Men Wash').

p. 148. Endre Ady, *A fekete zongora* ('The Black Piano'), translated by Adam Makkai; *A grófi szérűn* ('The Earl's Threshing Floor').

p. 156. Miklós Radnóti, *Második ekloga* ('Second Epilogue'), translated by George Gömöri and Clive Wilmer.

p. 159. János Pilinszky, *Quatran*, translated by Ted Hughes & János Csokits.

p. 191. Attila József, *Repedt kályhámon* ('On My Broken Stove'), translated by George Szirtes.

p. 206. Sándor Petőfi, *Egy gondolat* ('One Thought'), translated by George Szirtes.

p. 222. Árpád Tóth, *Lélektől lélekig* ('From Soul to Soul').

p. 227. Gyula Juhász, *Anna örök* ('Eternal Anna'), translated by George Szirtes.

p. 240. Mihály Vörösmarty, *Előszó* ('Prologue'), translated by Peter Zollman.

p. 240. Attila József, *Irgalom* ('Mercy') translated by George Szirtes.

p. 258. Attila József, *Ős patkány* ('An Ancient Rat') translated by John Bátki.

Hungarian books in translation (or not) that are mentioned in the text:

Endre Ady, *Poems*, introduction and translations by Anton N. Nyerges (Buffalo: Hungarian Cultural Foundation, 1969).

György Bálint, *A toronyőr visszapillant* ('The Lighthouse Keeper Looks Back'), (Budapest, Magvető 1966)

Mária Ember, *Hajtűkanyar*, ('Hairpin Bend') (Budapest: Szépirodalmi Könyvkiadó, 1974).

István Eörsi, *Emlékezés a régi szép időkre* ('Remembering the Good Old Times') (Budapest: Katalizátor Iroda, samizdat, 1988; Napra-forgó, 1st legal edition, 1989).

Ignác Goldziher, *Az iszlám* ('Muslim Studies'), edited by S.M. Stern, translated by C.R. Barber (originally published Budapest: 1881; Piscataway, NJ: Transaction Publishers, 2005).

Attila József, *The Iron-Blue Vault: Selected Poems*, translated by Zsuzsanna Ozsváth and Frederick Turner (Newcastle-upon-Tyne: Bloodaxe Books, 1999).

Attila József, *Poems*, edited by Thomas Kabdebo, translated by Michael Beevor, Michael Hamburger, Thomas Kabdebo, John Székely, Vernon Watkins (London: The Danubia Book Co., 1966).

Attila József, *Winter Night, Selected Poems*, translated by John Bátki (Budapest : Corvina, 1997).

Imre Kertész, *Fatelessness*, translated by Tim Wilkinson (New York: Alfred A. Knopf, 2004; London: Vintage, 2006).

Imre Kertész, *Kaddish for an Unborn Child*, translated by Tim Wilkinson (New York: Vintage, 2004; London: Vintage, 2010).

Imre Kertész, *Liquidation*, translated by Tim Wilkinson (New York: Alfred A. Knopf, 2004; London: Vintage, 2007).

Géza Komoróczy, Viktória Pusztai, Andrea Strbik, Kinga Frojimovics, *Jewish Budapest: Monuments, Rites, History* (Budapest: Central European University Press, 1995).

Dezső Kosztolányi, *Anna Edes*, translated by George Szirtes (Budapest: Corvina, 1991).

Dezső Kosztolányi, *Kornél Esti*, translated by Bernard Adams (New York: New Directions Publishing, 2010).

Dezső Kosztolányi, *Thirty-six Poems*, translated by Peter Zollman (Budapest: Maecenas, 2000).

Zsigmond Móricz, *Be Faithful Unto Death*, translated by Stephen Vizinczey (Budapest: Central European University Press, 1995).

Zsigmond Móricz, *Captive Lion*, translated by Bernard Adams (Budapest: Corvina 2011).

Péter Nádas, *A Book of Memories*, translated by Ivan Sanders and Imre Goldstein (New York: Farrar, Straus and Giroux, 1997).

Péter Nádas, *The End of a Family Story*, translated by Imre Goldstein (New York: Vintage, 2000).

Ana Novac, *The Beautiful Days of My Youth: My Six Months in Auschwitz and Plaszow*, translated by George L. Newman (New York: Henry Holt and Co., 1997).

János Pilinszky, *Passio*, translated by Clive Wilmer and George Gömöri (Tonbridge, Kent: Worple Press, 2011).

János Pilinszky, *The Desert of Love: Selected Poems*, translated by János Csokits and Ted Hughes (London: Anvil Press Poetry, 1989).

Miklós Radnóti, *Bori Notesz* ('Camp Notebook') in the Visible Poets Series, translated by Francis R. Jones (Todmorden, Lancs.: Arc Publications, 2000).

Miklós Radnóti, *Foamy Sky: The Major Poems of Miklós Radnóti* in the Lockert Library of Poetry in Translation, translated by Zsuzsanna Ozsváth and Frederick Turner (Princeton, NJ: Princeton University Press, 1992).

Miklós Radnóti, *Forced March*, translated by George Gömöri and Clive Wilmer (London: Enitharmon Press, 2004).

Miklós Radnóti, *Under Gemini: A Prose Memoir and Selected Poetry*, translated by Kenneth McRobbie (Budapest: Corvina Kiadó, 1985).

Jenő Rejtő, *The Blonde Hurricane*, translated by Istvan Farkas: http://mek.oszk.hu/01000/01022/index.phtml

Jenő Rejtő, *The 14-carat Roadster*, translated by Patricia Bozsó: http://mek.oszk.hu/01000/01021/index.phtml

Dezső Tandori, *Töredék Hamletnek* ('A Fragment for Hamlet'), 1968; *Egy talált tárgy megtisztítása* ('The Cleaning of a Found Object'), 1973. Some poems from these volumes might be found in: Dezső Tandori, *Birds and Other Relations*, translated by Bruce Berlind (Princeton: Princeton University Press, 1987).

Béla Zsolt, *Nine Suitcases*, translated by Ladislaus Löb (London: Pimlico, 2005).

There is a good multidimensional-multilingual web anthology, *Babelmatrix*, that displays both the original text and its translated version, and has a list of Hungarian works translated into English: http://www.babelmatrix.org/. Hungarian Literature Online provides information on Hungarian literature and presents new translations:
www.hlo.hu.